The Sociology
of
Contemporary India

The Sociology
of
Contemporary India

D. A. Chekki
University of Winnipeg

Foreword
RICHARD D. LAMBERT
University of Pennsylvania

South Asia Books

SOUTH ASIA BOOKS
Box 502, Columbia, Missouri 65201

ISBN 0 8364 0245 6

309.154
C 515 s

83-562

The Sociology of Contemporary India
© 1978, D.A. Chekki
First Edition 1978
Published by S.K. Ghai, Managing Director, Sterling Publishers Pvt. Ltd.,
AB/9 Safdarjung Enclave, New Delhi-16 for South Asia Books, Box 502,
Columbia, Missouri, 65201, USA.
Printed at Print India, Mayapuri, Industrial Area, Phase-1 New Delhi-110 064.

To our children
MAHANTESH and CHENAVIRESH
for the reasons those who
love them know

Foreword

Reviews of a discipline tend to be of two kinds. By far the most common kind involves a single scholar steeping himself or herself in the literature with greater or lesser diligence and comprehensiveness, distilling the major trends through the prism of his or her own professional biases. This exercise is usually accompanied by a set of prescriptions as to what the proper direction of the field might be; indeed, it often appears that the opportunity to lecture to others about what they ought to do in their research seems to be the principal reason for a review of the literature. These reviews are as good as —or as bad as—the professional skills of the analyst. The other kind of disciplinary review tries to present an aggregate cross-sectional view of the state of the collective enterprise with only a modest set of imperatives for the future. Professor Chekki's study is in the latter tradition, and, therefore, to me most welcome. It is often a sobering exercise to confront not what must be so but what is so. Professor Chekki's study actually classifies and counts the various contributions to Indian Sociology. The result is a much less monolithic picture than is usually painted. His subject bibliography alone is worth the price of the book; one wishes he had made it more extensive, perhaps as an appendix.

The second kind of review has its limitations too. There is no weighting system. The mediocre is counted along with the excellent. The boundaries drawn around our amorphous field and delineation of categories affect the count, and therefore the estimate of trends. And, above all, one misses the deft analysis that immediately illuminates a previously undetected latent trend in widely scattered publications. We all have our favourite concerns about the direction the field is taking. My current ones include surprise at the lack of attention in studies of the Indian family to 'intrafamily relations as against structural classifications and enumera-

(viii)

tions; the curious lack of attention to the popular culture—movies, popular songs, fashion, dress style, slang, folk heroes, etc.; the oversight in studies of social mobility of downward mobility and its consequences; the limited contributions to world sociology by Indian scholars on the subject of crowd behaviour—no society provides the variety and richness of detail on crowd phenomena as India does; the limited direct attention to the problem of how to induce millions of people to change their behaviour to effect changes in directions judged desirable by a few; and, above all, the strange reluctance—debates over the validity of American empiricism aside—to experiment with the new multivariate analytic techniques in a society that is exquisitely multivariate in its causation.

But we all have our own research agendas Professor Chekki allows the discipline to take its own way and spends his time ordering it retrospectively, drawing whatever empirical generalisations can be drawn from this process. It is a very healthy supplement to the first more oracular style of analysis. A follow-up symposium drawing on the enumerative data but somewhat more content oriented would be a welcome sequel to this useful analysis.

University of Pennsylvania
Philadelphia
14 July, 1978

RICHARD D. LAMBERT

Preface

Around the world, in recent years, there seems to be an efflo-
rescence of interest in the sociology of Sociology. Probably one of
the earliest efforts in this direction, on a massive worldwide scale,
was undertaken by Howard Becker and Harry Barnes in their
three-volume work *Social Thought from Lore to Science.* In the
late 1950's, J.S. Roucek edited a volume entitled *Contemporary
Sociology* which contained a review of trends in sociological research in several countries. A similar recent effort under the
editorship of R. Mohan and D Martindale resulted in a publication
called *Handbook of World Sociology.*

At the national level we have a series of publications reviewing
trends in Sociology in the United States. Among the several
volumes mention may be made of Robert Merton *et al.,* (eds.)
Sociology Today, and Talcott Parsons (ed.) *American Sociology.* It
is interesting to note that besides the USA, where Sociology
flourishes as a distinct discipline in institutions of higher learning,
other countries also have not lagged behind in terms of reporting
the status of Sociology. Besides numerous journal articles the
following booklength titles, a few among many, bear testimony to
this fact. *Sociology in Australia and New Zealand* by Baldock
and Lally, *Sociology in Britain* by Krausz, and *Sociology in Israel*
by Weller do provide an overview of trends in Sociology in these
countries.

In this regard sociology in India has received no less attention
(for details refer, Chapter 2 of this book). For those interested in
a detailed substantive, theoretical-methodological review of
Sociology in India a special mention should be made of *A Survey
of Research in Sociology and Social Anthropology* sponsored
by the Indian Council of Social Science Research. David Mandel-
baum's *Society in India* is another notable contribution. In a
series called *Main Currents in Indian Sociology* G.R. Gupta and

his associates deal with specific themes in greater depth. Rama-krishna Mukherjee's *Trends in Indian Sociology* was available when our book was already in the final stages of printing. Mukherjee attempts to provide a systematic answer to the 'what', 'how' and 'why' of Indian Sociology and, following from this, he tries to examine the questions about the 'what will it be' and 'what should it be' of Indian Sociology.

In content and approach *The Sociology of Contemporary India* departs from these trend reports in that it breaks new ground and sheds new light on hitherto unexplored aspects of sociology of India. This book deliberately avoids value-based discussion and it is seldom prescriptive. In this study we have attempted to provide a sociological reporting system and we have tried to establish social indicators that give us a measure of socio-logical research output. In this context this volume should be considered as a useful addition rather than a duplication of earlier efforts. For detailed bibliographic references of more than five thousand studies, on which the analyses of this book are based, the reader should refer to my earlier publication, *The Social System and Culture of Modern India*. Garland Publishing, Inc., New York & London, 1975, pp. xxv + 843.

This book neither advocates a sociology for India nor is it restricted to Sociology in India *per se*. The primary aim of this book is to present some emerging trends in the sociology of con-temporary India. Here is an attempt not only to present the major trends in each specialised area of sociological research but also to discuss their implications as well. Moreover, these trends are reviewed with the objective of evaluating the extent of gaps in sociological research so that researchers can direct their attention to areas and problems hitherto unattended or inadequately researched.

The second objective is to analyse the social characteristics, role and contribution of sociologists. In other words we focus on the sociology of sociologists. It is in this context we have looked at a related aspect of the sociology of publishing. In particular we have tried to examine how some endogenous and exogenous factors influence the pattern of publications that sociological research takes. Furthermore, we present some significant directions in regional studies. This leads us to a content analysis of journal articles in select subject areas. The final chapter deals with an international community of sociologists engaged in the study of the social system and culture of India.

This study is not specifically designed to answer those questions and problems that confront the sociology of knowledge. However, for those interested in the sociology of knowledge our review of trends in sociology provides some material for an enquiry into the relation between social structure and sociology.

The computer analysis portion of this study was undertaken at the University of Winnipeg Computer Centre. During my sabbatical year (1974-1975). I was a visiting research fellow at Karnatak University. It was during this period that I had the opportunity to work on this manuscript. Technically, this analysis is confined to a twenty-five year period beginning from 1947. Of course, since 1972 much water has flown under the bridge. An analysis of trends since that year is beyond the scope of this volume as it should constitute the content of another book. Nevertheless, the data and analysis presented in this book will serve as a basis for a comparative study of sociological research in different nations. This theme will constitute a major portion of a forthcoming volume.

It is our hope that in the meanwhile this quantitative representation of a quarter century of sociological research on India will aid researchers and policy-makers to recognise gaps in existing research and to establish priorities for further research. Obviously, the eventual purpose would be to create a sociological research 'balance sheet' that would be useful in setting new research goals and priorities and in clarifying policy choices for planning and funding new research projects.

During the last two decades of my teaching Sociology, among other research projects, I have pursued this research on the sociology of India. All these years I have benefited from the ideas of several scholars. Obviously, it is impossible to thank all of them. The references in this book provide a partial listing of these men and women. However, I would like to acknowledge here my indebtedness to a number of persons: to Professor Richard D. Lambert, the author of numerous publications and the editor of *The Annals of the American Academy of Political & Social Science*, for his thoughtful foreword; to Donna Krawetz for her research assistance in this project: to Professors K. Ishwaran, William A. Morrison, John R. Hofley, K. Chandrasekhar, and William K. Greenaway for their encouragement of and continuing interest in my academic work; to President Dr H.E. Duckworth, Dean Dr John Clake, and Dean Dr B.G. Hogg for their constant support of my research endeavours; and to all those scholars in India and abroad who responded to my enquiry. Thanks to my wife Sheela for her forbearance, encouragement, and insistence that from time to time I leave the research cell and join the world of family life. Finally, I appreciate the cooperation given me and the considerable interest expressed by Mr O.P. Ghai and his staff of Sterling Publishers in bringing out this book within a relatively short period of time.

DANESH A. CHEKKI

Department of Sociology
University of Winnipeg
30 June, 1978

Contents

Contents

The Sociology
of
Contemporary India

Introduction

Sociology in India has expanded rapidly since Independence (1947) as a separate branch of academic and practical knowledge. The discipline has been influenced by Western sociology and anthropology, notably that of the British and American. Despite strong pressures to conform to Western modes of sociological research, Indian sociology has developed an unique perspective of its own. It is the purpose of this analysis to examine Indian sociology as it has developed over the past twenty-five years (1947-1972) as a discipline which has adopted foreign elements but more importantly has evolved its own characteristics and emphases and peculiarities.

Such research can provide, with the advantage of hindsight, a sound basis for guiding future research. Once the progress of a particular discipline is documented gaps in research topics and methods become known and priorities may be set. Introspection by practitioners of a specific discipline as to their past efforts and accomplishments, therefore, is the basis for evaluation and deciding future directions. Once the past becomes documented and is related to the environment in which it existed, then the bounds on the minds and methods of researchers imposed because of that environment become clearer and may be overcome. Just as an individual must look inward from time to time, so must a scientific discipline. Only then can our past progress and limitations be charted in order that future courses of action be wisely taken.

Unfortunately, academic introspection by Indian sociologists in the past has generally been an exception rather than a rule. Those studies of the nature attempted here have been limited by biased data collection and by a tendency towards qualitative analysis. Micro-data banks, for example, drawn from only one or two journals, along with impressionistic statements rather than factual ones, have not yielded a comprehensive view of Indian sociology over any substantial length of time. Thus trend analyses for Indian sociological research have not only been few in number but also those that have been conducted have not used sufficient data or time perspective to draw a complete picture.

Recently, the Indian Council of Social Science Research has surveyed all important research work done so far in different fields of the Social Sciences. The survey work which has been published so far by the Council is very praiseworthy and will undoubtedly fulfil a vital function for priority setting by the Council as well as social scientists in general. The analysis presented here is not intended to be a duplication of the work of the ICSSR but proposes to approach the focus of study by asking different questions, using different methods and assuming a different perspective. Firstly, the basis of this analysis will be a large body of data collected from all branches of sociology. In contrast to this, the ICSSR has subdivided their analyses into the various sub-categories of sociology. Secondly, this analysis will manipulate data quantitatively followed by qualitative discussions of numerical findings and statistical tests which allow significant inferences to be drawn. Thirdly, the analysis presented here will entail the examination of variables not discussed by the ICSSR surveys such as types of publications (book, journals, etc.), place of publication, sex and number of authors and other factors.

The trend analysis presented here, however, has particular limitations. These limitations will be discussed in more detail as they occur in the body of the text but can be briefly mentioned here. The bulk of the data used has been drawn from bibliographic entries as the large number of pieces of research included did not permit the examination of every study in its complete form. The possibility of making errors when classifying data then is greatly increased from the probability that would occur if the actual work was used. The fact that any analysis of this nature relies on the classification of data also placed limitations on this study. The tabular results which will be presented, therefore, have some degree of error that is not measurable statistically, but has been controlled as far as possible.

Following a description of how data was collected and classified and a review of pertinent literature, the basic organisational framework of the analysis shall be a macro-analysis of data according to selected variables. The variables are time periods, subject area, nationality of authors, sex of authors, number of authors, type of publication, journals and regions. Quantitative data for each variable shall be presented followed by a discussion of findings. The macro-level analysis shall be followed by a point form summation of findings. A more indepth micro-level content analysis of journal articles from five important subject areas will then be presented which attempts to arrive at conclusions about other factors such as methodology and techniques of data collection, degree of quantification and theoretical developments. Once again quantitative data will be presented followed by discussion of results and a summation of major trends for each subject area. The final section is devoted to an analysis of empirical survey on the social and academic background of North American, Indian and European sociologists engaged in sociological studies of Indian society and culture.

ONE

Method of Data Collection and Classification

To begin the analysis of trends in sociolog.cal research in India over the past twenty-five years, a large body of data was collected. In all, 5226 entries that were considered contributions to Indian sociology were compiled in bibliographic form from the following sources:

(1) Sociological Abstracts
(2) South Asia : An Introductory Bibliography
(3) Books in Print
(4) Doctorates in Social Sciences awarded by Indian Universities up to 1967, for 1968, 1969 and 1970
(5) Doctorate Students in Social Sciences (India) (Parts 1 & 2) (Registered till 30 Sept.1969)
(6) American Doctoral Dissertations (since 1956)
(7) International Bibliography of Sociology
(8) Choice (1972)
(9) Current Sociology
(10) A Survey of Research in Sociology and Social Anthropology, ICSSR publication, vol.111, 1972
(11) Articles from relevant journals for 1972 (not included in latest sociological abstracts available)
(12) Chapters from books that do not deal solely with India and from edited books solely on India
(13) Numerous publishers' book lists
(14) Bibliographies from relevant books
(15) International Index to Periodicals

The resultant data was not the product of a statistically designed sample but was assumed to be a fairly accurate representation of research that has been undertaken from 1947 to 1972. Biases which have occurred in previous studies[1] have been eliminated by including a great number of journals as well as different publication forms such as books, research reports and others. Specialisation of journals and other publication forms then should not influence the results and produce indications of trends which do not exist in the whole body of sociological research.

Some types of entries have been excluded from this study because of the problems they presented. Bibliographies of government reports were not examined as they were not readily available, although several such entries were found in other sources. The coverage of government reports which contribute to sociological research in India is, however, probably incomplete. A very small number of studies were deleted because they were published in Indian languages and problems of translation did not allow important information to be recovered from the bibliographic entries.

The method of selection of Indian studies which was employed to collect the body of data for trend analysis was of advantage in that articles were considered which were not contained in sociological journals but nevertheless have made valid contributions to sociology. There were numerous entries of this nature which were found in journals that are indirectly related to sociology, for example; journals dealing with urban planning, public administration, industrial relations, political science and education.

Entries which were not strictly sociological in the sense of rigid, academic boundaries, were taken from the source material. For example, studies by political scientists, cultural anthropologists and economists were included if it was felt they contributed to the various specialised branches of sociology. Sociology is a broad discipline considering its subject areas or the phenomena it studies. Its uniqueness does not originate with the study of phenomena from the point of view of the phenomena but rather with the study of phenomena from the point of view of man's underlying social system or social life. Ideally the discipline, as a whole, should attempt to synthesize all aspects of phenomena of human social existence. Understanding the whole, however, is dependent on understanding the parts and vice versa and it is here that contributions from closely related disciplines become relevant to sociology and sociological findings are of value to other social sciences. It is here also that academic boundary lines become blurred and defy attempt at clear-cut delineations. It is not the purpose here to decide the disadvantages and advantages of this situation but to point out that the ambiguity of disciplinary boundaries justifies the inclusion of entries from related disciplines that appear to contribute to sociological research.

The foregoing discussion seems to apply especially to the case of India where sociology and cultural anthropology are often indistinguishable. For a long time sociology as an academic discipline could not enjoy an independent status in most Indian universities. Also quite early in Indian sociology there emerged an emphasis in mutualism in the human realm as well as an extension of this doctrine of symbiosis into the world of nature.[2] Thus as phenomena, both man-made and natural, are seen as being closely interrelated, it is reasonable to expect that the disciplines that study individual phenomena from different conceptual frameworks should be interrelated.

Because of the large number of entries, analysis that include all the data or a large part of it were necessarily reduced in scope only to consider the information which was readily obtainable from the bibliographic data. Each entry was coded according to variables describing subject area, date of publication, type of publication, place of publication, number of authors, nationality of author, sex of author, region studied and macro or micro-level perspective.

The subject classification and code chosen was that outlined in the *Sociological Abstracts* (1972) with some modifications. This classification system was chosen as it is quite comprehensive and well organised using major categories and sub-categories. Approximately, one-third of the data collected was from the *Sociological Abstracts*. Certain modifications were made to the classification system to render it more suitable to the kinds of entries being included as well as to separate more distinctly particular subject areas.

A sub-category was added for general works in social psychology that was mainly of the textbook variety and therefore did not belong to the more narrowly bounded *Sociological Abstracts'* sub-categories for Social Psychology. An addition of a sub-category containing entries that dealt with attitudes, prejudices, sentiments and motives was also made to Social Psychology in the hope of providing a more specific classification for these kinds of studies. Likewise, another sub-category was added for entries that attempted to focus on social problems broadly and as a result could not be included in the more restricted sub-categories under Social Problems and Social Welfare. A sub-category was created in the category of Demography and Human Biology for studies on family planning as this subject area appeared to form, using the number of entries as the criterion, a definite body of research. Research into the adoption process and innovations, if unrelated to family planning, was classified under the sub-category of Communications in Mass Phenomena. In most cases these entries had been classified under Rural Sociology by the *Sociological Abstracts* but again judging by the number of entries collected and giving precedence to the process of adoption and innovation over the nature of the innovations, that is, agricultural, it appeared beneficial to classify these entries more distinctly. The *Sociological Abstracts* have only one sub-category under Community Development, that being the sociology of communities and regions, which includes studies of communities and regions as well as research into community development as a particular process of change. For this analysis, regional and community studies were deleted from the category of Community Development and reclassified as belonging to Urban and Rural Sociology depending on the case. In this way, community development as a process of change was included in a category with no extraneous material to hamper more detailed analysis. Tribal Studies were classified as belonging to social anthropology. The resultant modified *Sociological Abstracts* classification scheme included twenty-eight categories and sixty sub-categories; it included all entries except those on mass culture, a sub-category of Mass Phenomena, and Radical Sociology.

The classification of bibliographic entries into subject area created some problematic situations. Firstly, as the *Sociological Abstracts* classification system has expanded in recent years entries from earlier years, in some instances, had to be reclassified. More important, however, was the problem encountered in attempting to classify entries from sources other than the *Sociological Abstracts* into subject areas only from the information provided by the titles. Titles may not indicate conclusively the main intention or aim of the author or the nature of the study. The problem was partially solved by locating some of the entries and examining them by relying on familiarity with the work in question from past usage and by noting the nature of the source from which the entry was drawn. For example, an entry drawn from a bibliography on tribal ethnography may have had an ambiguous title but the topic with which the bibliography dealt provided information with which a decision could be taken.

Classification into subject areas by the information contained in titles involves some amount of inaccuracy that has been avoided by more detailed consideration of each entry, but the method is also of value as titles generally are given to research findings with some thought and wish that they be as appropriate and explicit as possible in regard to authors' topical emphases. It is doubtful whether or not the time spent painstakingly obtaining over five thousand books, journal articles, reports, doctoral dissertations etc. and then researching each article to permit classification would be worth the added accuracy. It must also be borne in mind that any classification scheme of the kind employed here contains a degree of arbitrariness as to where lines can be drawn and the final aim is to reduce information into generalisations of varying degrees in the form of categories and sub-categories in order that a general overview of trends through time is obtained.

During the classification process operational definitions for each subject area was derived indirectly by examining the nature of articles classified into the various categories by the *Sociological Abstracts*. Decisions then were taken by example or precedence indicated in the *Sociological Abstracts* with an attempt to be consistent when considering similar entries. Ideally, classification should have taken place accompanied by lists of characteristics for each subject area. The likelihood of deriving such clear-cut definitions is however quite small due to the ambiguity present in sociology as to the exact nature of specialised branches. As one researcher, who experimented with studies that bear a similarity to this one, found; "Obstacles which stand in the way of (scientific journals) use in analysing developments in the field of sociology largely derive from the somewhat amorphous state of the field itself and the consequent lack of clearly defined analytical categories."[3]

The lack of clear-cut lines between subject areas led to the question of how to classify entries that appeared to make contributions to more than one subject area. Other researchers who have faced this problem have solved it by reading the entry to assess the author's main intention[4] or more concisely stated, the dependent variable in the study was identified and given more weight than the independent variables.[5] Because of the number and the inaccessibility of many entries, this study cross-classified entries and gave equal weight of both in case of a few overlapping subject areas. Cross-classification was felt to be appropriate as even if a study does give more emphasis to one particular subject area a contribution is also made to other areas.

The limitations of the classification scheme used here for subject area as well as its advantages have been clearly explained and the use of the scheme seems justifiable considering the inherent difficulties sociology presents. It is because of the problems encountered, however, that it must be clarified at the outset that attempting to pinpoint trends is at best a precarious undertaking, thus conclusions in a study of this nature must be drawn with caution and accompanied by a recognition of their tentativeness.

After classification by subject area the data was then coded and key punched on IBM cards and later transferred to magnetic tape for computer analysis into the following time periods ;

     1947-1952

     1953-1957

     1958-1962

     1963-1967

     1968-1972

     not known

A logical starting point for the study was 1947 as this was the year India gained her independence and presumably this meant a greater freedom and a new beginning in the undertaking of research in Indian universities. The newly formed government, with its commitment to planning, and realisation that changes in society caused by the plans must be measured, encouraged and financed sociological research in universities and research centres. The social sciences undertook the task of discovering how best to bring about the change of transforming a traditional society into one that was modern and industrialised.

It was believed that a breakdown of the twenty-five year period into five-year time segments would bring to light more clearly the changes that occurred without being too short to mask trends and allow for only very narrow generalisations.

The data was then classified according to the following publication forms :

(1) book
(2) book chapter
(3) doctoral dissertations completed or in progress
(4) government reports and census reports
(5) journal articles
(6) research reports, seminar readings
(7) not known

Noting publication form offered much potential information as to the main channels available to publish research findings and their utilisation.   The information was also considered valuable because it offered possibilities to help ascertain the role of different publication forms, for example, government reports and doctoral dissertations, besides facilitating the separation of particular types of research.   Each entry was considered only once as to publication form, the form it appeared in earliest taking precedence.

Place of publication was another kind of information obtainable from the bibliographic entries and this offered useful insights. Places of publication 'included categories such as India, North America, the United Kingdom, continental Europe and others such as Japan and Australia.   From this information it was hoped discoveries might be made as to the pattern of publication contributors to Indian sociology have adopted past and present. The information could possibly reveal the orientation of studies, that is, if they were of primary importance to Indians or if foreigners were also interested in them.   Information might also be indicated pertaining to publishing conditions in India for sociological research.   In some cases, especially for large publishing houses with branch offices in different countries, problems were encountered determining where entries had been published or if different sources indicated different places of publication.   In such instances the place where the entry was first published was used or if the entry had been published simultaneously in India and another country, India took precedence.

Classification of entries by number of authors was carried out according to the following format :

(1) one author
(2) two authors

(3) three or more authors

(6) government report

(5) not known

The information offered a means by which conclusions could be drawn regarding the extent of research teams in India, if research was conducted primarily by persons working alone and if these variables describing authorship have changed through time.

Noting the nationality of authors took place according to the following categories :

(1) Indian

(2) North American

(3) United Kingdom

(4) European

(5) Other

(6) In the case of joint or multiple authorship, at least one Indian

(7) In the case of joint or multiple authorship, where none are Indians

(8) Not known

It was hoped that the data for nationality would indicate which elements have dominated Indian sociology and the relative size of contributions from foreigners or non-Indians. Interesting results could also be obtained as to the change in the number of Indians and foreigners over the years. The classification where in the case of joint or multiple authorship, at least one Indian was taken as being an indication of international collaboration.

Classification of entries by authors' nationality produced diffi-culties as such information often is not readily known only by name, especially when attempting to distinguish between authors from North America and those from the United Kingdom. Lists of prominent scholars engaged in Indian sociological research and their nationality aided in this task as well as biographic data about authors accompanying their work. In spite of efforts to locate authors' nationality through these channels, 8.5% of the required information was not known. The 8.5% classed as unknown, however, included mainly non-Indians as Indian names generally were found to be more easily recognisable.

Information about authors was also gathered as to their sex in order to help ascertain the role women have played in Indian sociology as opposed to the number of males in research. Interesting comparisons then could be made between the number of foreign women and the number of Indian women, between male and female researchers in particular subject areas and between sex ratios in time periods. As in the case of nationality classification, classification of sex of authors was impeded by a lack of this information from the name alone. In some instances difficulties were encountered because many bibliographic entries from source material only included first name initials. The problem was partially solved by familiarisation with the sex of prominent Indian scholars and the practice of some publications to designate Miss or Mrs before female names.

To discover which parts of India have been the setting for most studies, entries were classified according to regional categories consisting of the states and union territories plus a number of broader designations such as South India and North India. The majority of titles did not specifically name the state within which the studies fell but more often contained the name of a particular village, town, district or tribal group. In these cases places were located on maps or for tribal groups, social anthropological works dealing with the distribution of groups throughout India were consulted. In cases where tribal groups were spread over a number of states broader regional classes were used. The broader regional classes were also used when they were included in titles. If these attempts at finding the location of tribal groups or places were not successful then the actual study and its description in the *Sociological Abstracts* were consulted when possible. Studies that were not regional in nature, for example, those in theory and methodology, were designated as much as were those studies which dealt with all of India or the regional category was not known.

References

1. Imtiaz Ahmad, "Note on Sociology in India," *The American Sociologist*, November, 1966, p. 245.

2. Howard Becker and Harry Elmer Barnes, "Sociology in India, China and Japan," *Social Thought From Lore to Science*, vol. 3, (New York: Dover Publications, Inc., 1961) p. 1146.

3. Helen G. Tibbitts , "Research in the Development of Sociology: A Pilot
   Study in Methodology," *American Sociological Review*, 27, p. 892.
4. John H. Barnsely, "On the Sociology of Values: Patterns of Research," *The
   Sociological Review*, 20, 2, 1972, p. 230.
5. Tibbitts, op. cit., p. 893.

TWO

Review of Literature

A review of literature analysing trends in Indian sociological research indicates that certain common beliefs have emerged as well as differences of opinion. Arguments have been presented over the actual presence of particular trends and over the value of different avenues of research.   In spite of the interesting and important conclusions these studies have reported with a few exceptions, they do not constitute a significant field of enquiry in Indian sociology. The classification system used for this analysis distinguished publications on the history, present state and theory of sociology in India.[1] The following table illustrates the comparative lack of trend research :

TABLE 1

Time Period	Number of Publications	% of Total Number of Publications
1947-1952	6	1.8%
1953-1957	15	2.8
1958-1962	30	3.1
1963-1967	42	2.9
1968-1972	70	3.7
1947-1972	163	3.1%

The absolute number of publications included in the category has increased greatly since 1947 but relative to the rest of the output in sociological research, the percentage of publications has increased only by 1.9%. Comparison with the results from a study on British sociology from 1950 to 1970 analysing articles published in three British sociological journals and using the same classification system, makes clear the Indian shortage. In the British investigation 16.3% of the total number of articles fell into the category.[2] There is the possibility that the British study defined the category differently but even then the discrepancy between the figures, 16.3% and 3.1%, is quite large. The difference then, is not only a result of possible variations in definition but also indicates that compared to British sociology, Indian sociology is lacking with respect to trend analysis.

The contributors to sociological trend research have been primarily of Indian descent; to name but a few, mention can be made of I. Ahmed, G.C. Hallen, T.N. Madan, K. Motwani, R. Mukherjee, M.N. Srinivas, R.N. Saxena, S.C. Dube, Vidyarthi, and A.K. Saran. Valuable insights have also come from foreign authors such as F.G. Bailey, Marshall B. Clinard, Joseph W. Elder, T.B. Bottomore, L. Dumont and D. Pocock. The state of sociology in India in the past has been examined as to theoretical frameworks, subject area concentrations and techniques and methods of data collection and analysis. Attention has been given to the implantation of sociology in Indian universities and the development of its teaching as a distinct subject.

Besides the contribution from scholars working independently the progress of sociological research in India has been monitored by conference addresses and proceedings and more recently the Indian Council of Social Science Research. Formed in 1969, the ICSSR has made it an objective "to review the progress of social science research and to give advice to its users in government or outside."[3] In the future it can be expected that the ICSSR will become a major contributor to trend analysis as it is already fulfilling this role evidenced by the numerous articles dealing with trends in the ICSSR Newsletter. The ICSSR has also undertaken the Survey of Research in Social Sciences initiated in 1969-70. The Survey hopes to ascertain work done so far, to determine trends and to point out areas that have been neglected. The ICSSR so far has published three volumes and these reports are being used to determine priorities and policies for the ICSSR support for programmes of research.

Indian sociology has been shaped by many forces both indigenous and external to India. Forces indigenous to India in the form of social and religious traditions have had great impact on the development of Indian sociology. The traditions of India have given her people a common intellectual heritage that enters into every facet of life. From Hinduism a model of the human social system is obtained that fits into the larger system and fundamental laws of nature and ultimately the entire cosmos. As religion is the centre around which social life revolves and the fact the religious beliefs form a mode of life, religious traditions are of focal point for the study of Indian society.

Because Indian life, especially in the past has been characterised by this blending of spiritualism into everyday life, traditional Indian sociology has taken on a philosophical, metaphysical and theological tone and cannot be according to R.N. Saksena, entirely 'objective' in its content and approach.[4] Traditional Indian sociology has therefore been more of a social philosophy that is based on a foundation where "what is organic in Nature and shapes her end blindly and haphazardly becomes purposive in human society, and thus the pattern of life, spiritually and teleologically progressive, crosses boundaries of time and space."[5]

Traditional Indian thought, however, has been subjected to the influence of forces external to India and forces within India in the form of social and economic change. These forces, that have changed Indian society in a variety of ways, have led to a diversification of approaches in studying Indian society. The approaches that have been taken towards studying Indian society as it comes to feel the pressures of external forces and the forces of change are generally agreed upon by those that have researched the progress of Indian sociology. Differences of opinion have arisen though over more detailed aspects of the nature of trends and over the value of particular approaches in the past and for the future.

T.B. Bottomore[6] in an article entitled "Sociology in India" published in 1962 discerns three major trends in Indian sociological research. A few years later Imtiaz Ahmad[7] in a rebuttal to another article on sociology in India by M.B. Clinard and J.W. Elder,[8] based his arguments on Bottomore's analysis but elaborated on it considerably.

Ahmad in "Note on Sociology in India" discerns four different trends in Indian sociology. The first trend is called 'philosophical.'

Sociologists following this approach have concerned themselves directly with logical and methodological problems. The aim has been to develop a sociological theory that is closely linked to traditional Indian history and social thought. Their emphasis on traditional Indian thought however has not made them narrow in their outlook as they are fully acquainted with Western ideas but reject sociological positivism. Instead of revising the logic and method of sociology, their efforts are directed towards restating moral and religious practices which underlie social order in India.

Ahmad points out a second trend of Indological studies. This trend is characterised by attempts to understand modern Indian society through facts and explanations taken from Indian scriptures and legal historical documents. Reconstruction of Indian social history uses "uncritical Victorian anthropology and coupled with the use of ancient texts, this trend seems a strange blend of old-fashioned ethnology and classical Indology."

Thirdly, a trend is distinguished that is 'social anthropological'. Social anthropology in India has been responsible for many field studies. They have helped dispell the book-view of Indian society produced by the study of Indian society on the basis of religious and legal literature. In recent years social anthropological studies have produced an impressive body of data on different aspects of Indian social structure.

A fourth trend Ahmad mentions is not a coherent body of thought but more a general attitude of approval toward acceptance of American sociological thought and scientific research techniques. The American influence, according to Ahmad has not really been put into practice. Terms have been borrowed and used but actual studies involving hypotheses formulation and testing and statistical research techniques have been limited.

T.B. Bottomore in "Sociology in India" states all three trends but he does not specifically mention the Indological trend and makes efforts to clarify the social anthropological trend. Bottomore makes mention of the British influence in respect to the Indian preference for the social anthropological outlook. The fact that British social anthropology had more intellectual liveliness than British sociology and India in the past had been intellectually dependent on Britain accounts for the implantation of the trend in India. The social anthropological approach was also adhered to because it offered a very suitable method for investigating Indian phenomena such as tribal groups and small villages. The social anthropological approach however has been the cause of the neglect of many contemporary problems within urban and industrial India.

The relevance of village studies of the anthropological type has been seriously questioned in regard to formulating a general body of theory. Social anthropological studies tend to be microcosmic in approach. R.N. Saksena[9] and A.K. Saran[10] in reports on sociology in India point out that these studies have attempted to make generalisations about Indian society that are unwarranted because they have been induced from insufficient data even in light of contrary evidence. Generalisations are also invalid because the time spent gathering data, six to eighteen months, is not long enough for proper appraisal and understanding.

Clinard and Elder, two Americans who analysed Indian sociology within the framework of the sociology of knowledge, agree with Bottomore that the predilection for anthropological field studies has led to an undesirable paucity of urban studies. Ahmad points out, contrary to this view, that the rural emphasis is justified in India because almost 80% of the population is rural and the information is needed for the Community Development Programme. Ahmad goes on to state that the importance of urban studies has not been ignored and studies of urban social life are being increasingly undertaken.

The American influence on Indian sociology does not constitute as clear a trend as the British influence characterised by social anthropology. Clinard and Elder contend, from an analysis based on articles from the *Sociological Bulletin* that "western" empirical methods have been rejected by Indian sociologists because of reservations about the applicability of these foreign techniques to Indian society. Clinard and Elder instead emphasize the use of historical-religious materials to understand the present.

Ahmad does not agree with Clinard and Elder and argues that their judgement has been biased by the journal that they analysed. Ahmad conducted a similar analysis using articles from *The Eastern Anthropologist* and *The Economic Weekly* and found that Indian sociology is predominantly empirically oriented. The comments of several other Indian sociologists seem to support Ahmad in that they bewail the ready acceptance many younger scientists have for imported, modern techniques and approaches.

P. Chakrabarti[11] undertook an interesting study in 1970 entitled "Quantification and Social Research : A Trend Analysis." He found that 71% of the 3907 publications he had drawn from six libraries were non-quantitative in that no sampling or research design was used to collect data and subsequent analysis was purely non-quantitative. It was also brought to light that foreigners working in India are not more quantitatively oriented than Indians. This study leads to the conclusion that although Indian sociology has moved towards empiricalism as witnessed by Ahmad's study, modern scientific techniques from abroad are not being used widely. Chakrabarti states that in a country as vast as India it is impossible to correctly interpret the diverse social phenomena simply by statistical logic without qualitative knowledge of the nature of societal problems. He also takes care to remark though, that as fruitful as descriptive studies have been, quantification for specific types of analysis can be an aid in arriving at more definite conclusions. The philosophical trend and the Indological trend mentioned earlier are definite trends within Indian sociological research that seem to represent a divergence of opinion over (American) empiricalism and (British) social anthropology and traditional Indian social thought. J.P. Suda for example emphasises the need to study the ancient literature of India as it is "full of matter of great value to the study of sociology."[12] Suda believes that a reliance on Western thought cannot lead to an indepth understanding of Indian society and for this reason Indians should turn to their own thinkers for inspiration and guidance and consult the wealth of knowledge contained in ancient literature. R.N. Saksena also seems to be an adherent to this line of thought and directs his criticism towards village studies using the ethnographic approach. As these studies interpret traditional society in terms of the assumptions of modern thought, Saksena believes that tradition is not being understood in its proper perspective. Clinard and Elder clearly point out this trend in Indian sociology and remark that not an insignificant number of Indian scholars believe that understanding of Indian society today can only be obtained if one is familiar with past languages and literature.

S.C. Dube[13] views sociology as having a fundamental role within the development of India. As one of India's major weaknesses in social research, he cites the refusal to examine social reality empirically by seeking to find answers to modern problems in ancient texts and traditions. The result is a body of research that has about it an air of unreality, scientists becoming commentators and at times, glorifiers of the past.

A review of literature reveals then that although some trends have emerged in Indian sociology, the magnitude or influence of trends is debatable as also the value of particular trends. Ahmad recognises this divergence of opinions and states that sociology in India is characterised by different theoretical tendencies. The problem of determining trends in sociology and then deciding their values are present in every country but are especially compounded in India by disputes over ancient and modern learning and traditional and modern society. Disputes are also present over the validity of applying research techniques from foreign countries as some sociologists believe Indian society requires special approaches whereas others believe understanding can be reached without the formulation of unique Indian tools.

S.K. Nandy[14] postulates that Indian sociology in the future will begin to blend traditional trends with the more scientific-positivistic outlook from the West. This view of sociology sees Indian society as being a synthesis of traditional elements and modern elements; therefore sociology will eventually reflect this blending of forces within a society in transition.

References

1. Examples of publications classified in this category are: R. Mukherjee, "Empirical Social Research on Contemporary India," *Social Science Information*, 8, 6, 1969, pp. 69-83.
   A. K. Saran, "For a Sociology of India," *Eastern Anthropologist*, 15, 1, 1962, pp. 53-68.
   S. P. Nagendra, "The Concept of Ritual in Modern Sociological Theory," Doctoral Dissertation, Agra University, 1968.
2. Peter Collison and Susan Webber, "British Sociology 1950-1970: A Journal Analysis." *The Sociological Review*, 19, 4, 1971, p. 538.
3. J. P. Naik, *Role, Responsibilities, Functions, Programmes and Organization of the ICSSR*, Occasional Monographs, (New Delhi: ICSSR, 1971), p. 1.
4. R. N. Saksena, "Some Observations on Sociology In India," *The American Sociological Review*, 27, p. 97.
5. Howard Becker and Harry Elmer Barnes, "Sociology in India, China and Japan," *Social Thought From Lore to Science*, vol. 3, (New York: Dover Publications, Inc., 1961), p. 1147.

6. T. B. Bottomore, "Sociology in India," *British Journal of Sociology*, 13, 2, June 1962, pp. 98-106.

7. Imtiaz Ahmad, "Note on Sociology in India," *The American Sociologist*, 1, 5, Nov. 1966, pp. 244-47.

8. M. B. Clinard and J. W. Elder, "Sociology in India: A Study in the Sociology of Knowledge", *American Sociological Review*, 30, 4, Aug., 1965, pp. 581-587.

9. Saksena, op. cit., p. 98.

10. A. K. Saran, "India", *Contemporary Sociology*, edited by J. S. Roucek, New York : Greenwood Publishers, 1969) p. 1028.

11. P. Chakrabarti, "Quantification and Social Research : A Trend Analysis" *The Economic Weekly*, 5, 38, 1970, pp. 1571-75.

12. J.P. Suda "The Teaching of Sociology in India," *Indian Journal of Social Research*, 8, 1, 1967, p. 27.

13. S.C. Dube, "The Role of Social Sciences", *ICSSR Newsletter*, III, June 1972 pp. 3-10.

14. Santosh Kumar Nandy, "A Note on Sociology in India vis-a-vis Sociology in the West", *Indian Sociological Bulletin*, 3, 2, Jan. 1966, pp. 171-175.

THREE

Major Trends in Indian Sociological Research: Subject Area

In order to ascertain major trends within Indian sociological research frequency counts were obtained for each variable for each five-year time period and for the total twenty-five years. These frequency counts shall be presented in tabular form arranging variables in rank order from highest to lowest frequency for 1947-72 and giving absolute and relative frequencies. In some cases data shall also be presented through the use of graphs. Following this quantitative presentation, an attempt shall be made to discuss the findings from a qualitative point of view. For the discussion of major trends in specific subject areas examples of the types of studies being referred to are contained in footnotes. The majority of these examples have been chosen because they seem to be representative and, unless specifically stated, are not to be taken as being the most important work in a particular field.

The most obvious trend that has emerged is the greatly increased productivity of Indian sociological research. From Table 2 it is evident that the number of studies has increased by almost 600% since the first five-year time period until the last. Over one-third of the sociological research for twenty-five years has been published in the last five years. This great increase in research output is perhaps partially due to the fact that better bibliographic coverage exists for later years therefore a disproportionate amount of more recent studies have been inadvertently included. As the *Sociological Abstracts* did not start publication until 1953 it is highly possible that many journal articles relevant to this study published from 1947 to 1952 have been omitted. The magnitude of the increase however, cannot be totally accounted for by these possible biases; therefore, in fact, Indian sociological research has increased dramatically in productivity.

TABLE 2

Indian Sociological Research, 1947-72: Absolute and Relative Frequencies of Number of Studies in Five-Year Time Periods

Date of publication	Number of studies	Relative frequency
1968—1972	1911	36.6%
1963—1967	1501	28.6
1958—1962	944	18.1
1953—1957	527	10.1
1947—1952	323	6.2
not known	20	.4
Total (1947-1972)	5226	100%

Several reasons for the increase in productivity can be mentioned briefly and shall be discussed later in more detail. Since Independence (1947) Indian universities generally have expanded in facilities and enrolment. Sociology has attracted its share of students from this burgeoning of post-secondary education. Sociology has come to be recognised as an independent field of research in Indian universities instead of a branch of other social sciences. Because of widespread social problems and the tasks which face the government of bringing about social change and economic development, many research centres and universities have been financed to undertake sociological research. The number of foreign sociologists conducting sociological research in India has also tended to increase after Independence.

SUBJECT AREA

The most highly researched area in Indian sociology, according to this analysis, is Culture and Social Structure. Although the category has declined sharply since the first time period, it still holds the most prominent position.

TABLE 3

Indian Sociological Research, 1947-1972: Cell Frequencies in per cent and Number and Rank Order by Subject Classification

Subject Categories	1947-52	1953-57	1958-62	1963-1967	1968-72	1947-72	% Change 1947-52 to 1968-72
1	2	3	4	5	6	7	8
I Culture and Social Structure	21.1% (68)	18.8% (131)	14.7% (139)	11.6% (175)	10.1% (193)	12.9% (678)	−11.0%
II Social Differentiation	7.1 (23)	10.4 (55)	7.9 (74)	6.6 (99)	10.4 (198)	8.6 (451)	+ 3.3
III Rural Sociology	10.2 (33)	8.5 (45)	6.1 (58)	9.8 (147)	8.1 (154)	8.4 (438)	− 2.1
IV The Family & Socialisation	4.0 (13)	8.2 (43)	7.8 (74)	7.8 (118)	7.4 (142)	7.5 (390)	+ 3.4
V Social Change and Economic Development	4.9 (16)	4.9 (26)	5.5 (52)	6.2 (83)	7.5 (143)	6.3 (331)	+ 2.6

Subject Area							
VI Demography and Human Biology	1.8 (6)	7.4 (39)	8.5 (80)	5.6 (83)	5.2 (99)	6.0 (307)	+ 3.4
VII Mass Phenomena	3.7 (12)	3.3 (18)	4.4 (42)	8.8 (131)	5.5 (94)	5.8 (307)	+ 1.3
VIII Political Interactions	8.0 (26)	4.0 (21)	3.1 (29)	5.6 (85)	5.7 (110)	5.2 (272)	− 2.3
IX Social Problems and Social Welfare	3.3 (11)	4.2 (22)	6.0 (57)	3.9 (58)	5.7 (110)	4.9 (259)	+ 2.4
X Complex Organisations	4.3 (14)	7.3 (38)	4.8 (45)	3.9 (59)	4.9 (93)	4.8 (253)	+ .6
XI Social Psychology	5.8 (19)	2.2 (11)	3.1 (30)	3.3 (49)	4.4 (86)	3.7 (195)	− 1.4
XII Sociology of Education	2.2 (7)	4.2 (22)	3.0 (28)	4.7 (70)	3.1 (59)	3.6 (187)	+ .9
XIII Community Development	—	1.1 (6)	4.1 (39)	4.7 (71)	3.2 (62)	3.4 (180)	+ 3.2
XIV Urban Sociology	3.7 (12)	2.3 (12)	4.8 (45)	2.7 (41)	3.5 (66)	3.4 (178)	− .2
XV Sociology: History and Theory	1.8 (6)	2.8 (15)	3.1 (30)	2.9 (42)	3.7 (70)	3.1 (164)	+ 1.9

TABLE 3 (*Contd.*)

1	2	3	4	5	6	7	8
XVI Sociology of Religion	5.9 (19)	2.5 (13)	3.0 (28)	2.7 (41)	1.7 (37)	2.6 (135)	− 4.2
XVII Group Interaction	3.7 (12)	1.3 (7)	1.3 (12)	1.7 (25)	1.9 (37)	1.8 (93)	− 1.8
XVIII Sociology of Health and Medicine	.6 (2)	2.9 (15)	1.9 (18)	1.7 (25)	1.6 (29)	1.7 (89)	+ 1.0
XIX Social Control	1.5 (5)	.8 (4)	1.5 (14)	1.3 (19)	1.7 (23)	1.5 (75)	+ .2
XX Sociology of the Arts	2.7 (9)	1.5 (8)	1.2 (11)	1.3 (20)	1.2 (22)	1.4 (71)	− 1.5
XXI Methodology and Research Technology	1.2 (4)	.6 (3)	2.1 (20)	1.5 (22)	1.3 (24)	1.3 (73)	+ .1
XXII Planning Forecasting and Speculation	.9 (3)	.8 (4)	.8 (8)	.7 (10)	.7 (14)	.7 (40)	+ .2
XXIII Sociology of Knowledge	.3 (1)	.2 (1)	.3 (3)	.5 (8)	.6 (10)	.4 (23)	+ .3

XXIV Sociology of Science	.6 (2)	—	.3 (3)	.4 (6)	.4 (7)	.3 (18)	—	.2
XXV Studies in Poverty	—	—	.4 (4)	.1 (1)	.4 (7)	.2 (12)	+	.4
XXVI Environmental Interactions	—	—	.1 (1)	.1 (1)	.2 (3)	.1 (5)	+	.2
XXVII Studies in Violence	—	—	—	.1 (1)	.1 (2)	.1 (3)	+	.1
Total	100% (323)	100% (527)	100% (944)	100% (1501)	100% (1911)	100% 5206*		

*Date of publication was not known for twenty entries.

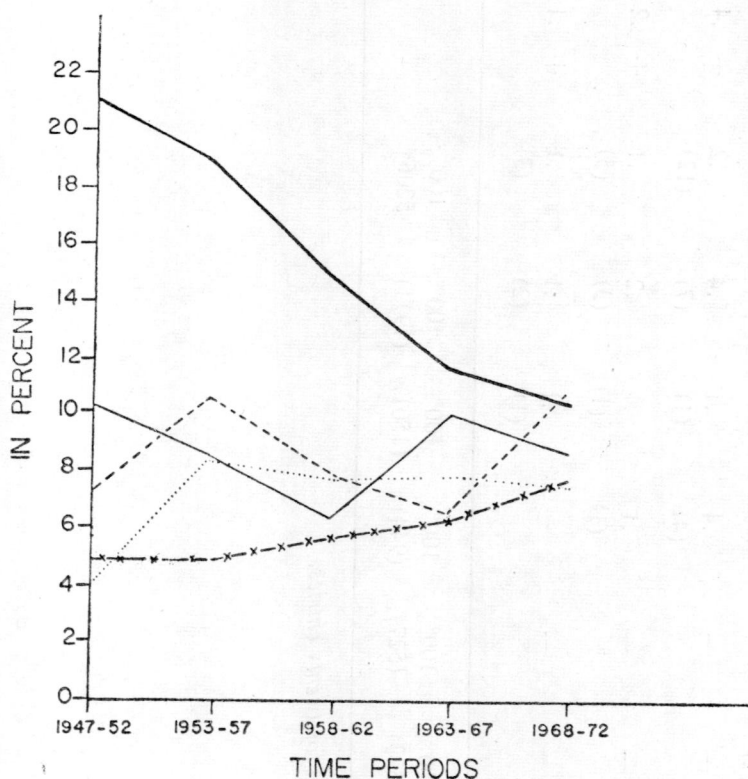

GRAPH I

Indian Sociological Research; 1947 - 72: Frequency
Distribution of the Five Most Researched Subject Categories
By Time Periods.   ━━━━ Culture & Social Structure
                     ────── Rural Sociology
                     ------ Social Differentiation
                     ...... The Family & Socialization
                     ─x──x─ Social Change & Economic Development

The sub-category of social organisation has remained relatively constant in output throughout the twenty-five year period. Some changes though have taken place in the kinds of research being undertaken. In the earliest two periods studies of tribal organisation, kinship and social structure were very prevalent.[1] There was also a substantial number of works which examined Hindu kinship, organisation, social order and the foundations of these aspects of Indian society. Of notable mention are I. Karve's *Kinship Organization in India*,[2] K.M. Kapadia's *Hindu Kinship*[3] and P. Prabhu's *Hindu Social Organization*.[4] In later time periods these topical emphases have not changed or diminished in number but new problems and aspects of social organisation in India have been studied. More attention has been paid to the changes taking place in social structure, and studies on impact of modernising forces on the roles of older people, peasant communities, caste and kinship.[5] Tribal and clan organisation and kinship have still been the subject of study but in addition to these, investigations have been carried out of the social structure of non-tribal villages and some aspects of social organisation of religious groups such as Moslems. The social structure and social interrelations among different caste-groups of the same village have been studied, usually using a small-scale single village approach, although there have also been a few studies using a comparative approach. Research has been done in the study of kinship, for example in measuring kinship orientation and examining inter-kin marriage and kinship cohesiveness.[6] Research activity has also been centred on the study of social structure and kinship networks in ancient India and the social structure of British society in pre-Independence India.

The sub-category of culture has declined by 2%. Studies in culture have not changed that greatly in problems studied. Since 1947 there has been a great amount of interest in tribal cultures and changes they have undergone as a result of cultural contact and modernisation.[7] Studies have been conducted which examine different religious cults within India and their cultural milieu. The cultural process or the formation of cultural patterns in India has been investigated.[8] Some researchers have tried to view the Indian people as a synthesis of many cultures and races, discussing cultural unity in spite of the apparent diversity and on the other hand, cultural conflicts and the need for and process of cultural integration.[9] There has been a sustained interest in culture and social

TABLE 4

Subject Category and Sub-categories	1947-52	1953-57	1958-62	1963-67	1968-72	1947-72	% Change 1947-52 to 1968-72
I Culture and Soc. Structure	21.1% (68)	18.8% (131)	14.7% (139)	11.6% (175)	10.1% (193)	12.9% (678)	—11.0%
(a) social organisation	2.5 (8)	4.4 (23)	2.3 (22)	2.5 (38)	2.5 (47)	2.6 (138)	0
(b) culture (evolution)	5.0 (16)	5.5 (29)	5.1 (48)	2.9 (44)	3.0 (58)	3.7 (195)	— 2.0
(c) social anthropology (& ethnology)	13.6 (44)	8.9 (47)	7.3 (69)	6.2 (93)	4.6 (88)	6.6 (345)	— 9.0

TABLE 5

Subject Category and Sub-categories	1947-52	1953-57	1958-52	1963-67	1968-72	1947-72	% Change 1947-52 to 1968-72
II Social Differentiation	7.1 (23)	10.4 (55)	7.9 (74)	6.6 (99)	10.4 (198)	8.6 (451)	+3.3
(a) social stratification	6.5 (21)	9.5 (50)	6.4 (60)	5.5 (82)	7.4 (141)	6.8 (355)	+.9
(b) sociol. of occup. & prof.	.6 (2)	.9 (5)	1.5 (14)	1.1 (17)	3.0 (57)	1.8 (96)	+2.4

life in different times in Indian history and in traditional values and culture as a background to modern India.

The sub-category of social anthropology has experienced by far the greatest relative decline in frequency and has fallen from first in rank in 1947-52 to sixth in 1968-72. Types of research activity generally have not changed. Most studies have been conducted in the tribal setting or in small villages.[10] There has been much interest in the particular rituals, ceremonies, rites and festivals of villages.[11] A few studies especially in more recent years but also earlier have addressed themselves to different topics such as changes tribes are undergoing, social attitudes among tribes and the socio-economic implications of rituals.[12] Recently, social and cultural anthropologists have reassessed their role in social science research and established problems to which they should give priority. This re-evaluation of the direction social anthropology should be taking will probably change the nature of social anthropological studies towards a greater emphasis on traditional forms and processes that are rapidly being transformed.[13]

The second most highly researched area is Social Differentiation which mainly includes studies on different aspects of the caste system and research into the sociology of occupations and professions. The category has increased by 3.3% since the first five-year period to the last period, this increase being due to a slight increase in social stratification and a larger increase in the sociology of occupations and professions (see Table 5). The caste system, as would be expected, has been a major concern of Indian sociological research. In past years studies dealing with the origins and development of caste[14] held most researchers' attention but in more recent years, as Indian society itself has undergone changes, caste has been studied in light of its present day dynamics. Social Differentiation or more specifically the caste system has been the subject of many important sociological works such as G.S. Ghurye's *Cast and Class in India*,[15] and *Caste Class and Occupation*,[16] A.M. Hocart's *Caste : A Comparative Study*,[17] L. Dumont's *Homo Hierarchicus*,[18] J. H. Hutton's *Caste in India*,[19] C. Bougle's *Essays on the Caste System*, M. N. Srinwas's *Caste in Modern India and Other Essays*[21] and *Castes: Old and New*[22] by A. Betille.

Studies about the changing role of women and their status have also been the focus of more attention in recent years. Many of these works have been the product of female authors. Examples of such studies are *Changing Status of Women in Post-Independence India*[23] by C.A. Hate, *Changing Status of Women In Hindu Middle Class Society*[24] by N. Gupta, *Indian Women in Transition* : *A Bangalore Case Study*[25] by R.L. Goldstein and *The Life of Women In a Village of North India* : *A Study of Role and Status*[26] by M.S. Luchinsky.

The increase in the sociology of occupations and professions is understandable considering changes taking place in Indian society, where old barriers to social position and occupation are gradually being eroded. In approximately the two earliest periods, research was more concerned with occupational surveys of particular places or the socio-economic conditions of particular occupational groups.[27] In the later three periods a shift is evident towards more research into social and occupational mobility and job aspirations and satisfaction.[28]

Another distinct interest has emerged into aspects of the new elites in India that are distinguished by occupation not caste grouping   Studies of the social origins and social structure of Indian legislators, lawyers, and managers have been conducted.[29] Likewise, research has included the study of the emergence and nature of an Indian middle class as defined in terms of occupation, for example white-collar workers.   The role and conditions of India's academic elite have also been examined and recently investigations have been made into the problems of unemployment among certain professionals in India such as engineers and their exodus, along with other scientists, to more "attractive" foreign countries such as the United States.[30]

Rural Sociolagy is another important area in Indian sociological research although in recent years it has declined somewhat in relation to other subject areas, that is, by 2.1% as shown in Table 3 (p. 24). Rural sociology, in some respects, has not changed that drastically in approach. In the early periods, studies in Rural Sociology were mainly of the socio-economic survey type that assumed a microcosmic approach, although some research was also directed towards rural development and rural pilot projects.[31] In more recent years the micro village studies have persisted but in addition to these there is research into changing social patterns in the rural setting, the effect of agricultural (rural community) development programmes, the effects of urbanization on rural life and the development of rural industry.[32] Rural sociology appears to be filling the need of government and planners for information as to how programmes are working and how they could be improved but comparative studies are lacking between villages within India and with villages outside of India. Most of these village studies, largely descriptive in nature, rarely make significant contributions to sociological theory.

The category of the Family and Socialization has increased since the earliest period, 1947-1952, by 3.4% (Table 6). The frequencies of sub-categories reveal that research into the family itself accounted for almost half of the increase and the other fields of the sociology of the child and socialization, adolescence and youth and the sociology of sexual behaviour accounted for the rest of the increases. These other fields constituted new avenues of research that Indian sociology has taken since the early 1950's In earlier periods but also continuing into recent years, emphasis has been placed on examination of family types and their structure of composition[33] and marriage customs,[34] especially of tribal groups. Since approximately the late 1950's however more attention has been directed towards changes that are effecting family life,[35] for example, the impact of education and urbanization on attitudes towards the traditional family.

These studies have often been indepth reports based on data gathered in the field by sampling and surveys such as M.S. Gore's *Urbanization and Family Change*[36] and A.D. Ross's *The Hindu Family In Its Urban Setting.*[37] K.M. Kapadia in the first edition of *Marriage and Family In India*[38] in 1955 approached the subject of the Hindu family differently, drawing data from sacred literature of Hindu Law. In later editions however, empirical analyses of contemporary problems of the Hindu family such as in urban areas were added. The behaviour of different sexes and age groups within the family is being examined as investigation has taken place into the changing role of women in the family context[39] and the changing ideas of young people which cause inter-generational conflict. Changing age at marriage and changing attitudes towards inter-caste marriage constitute other fields of research activities.[40] The Family and Socialization appears to be richer than other fields in cross-cultural comparisons between families in different regions of India and between families in India and those in other countries.[41]

TABLE 6

Subject Category and Sub-categories	1947-52	1953-57	1958-62	1963-67	1968-72	1947-72	% Change 1947-52 to 1968-72
IV Family and Socialization	4.0 (13)	8.2 (43)	7.8 (74)	7.8 (118)	7.4 (142)	7.5 (390)	+ 3.4
(a) soc. of child & socialization	—	.6 (3)	.6 (6)	.9 (13)	.6 (11)	.6 (33)	+ .6
(b) adolescence and youth	.3 (1)	.2 (1)	.3 (3)	.7 (11)	1.0 (19)	.7 (35)	+ .7
(c) soc. of sexual behaviour	—	.6 (3)	.4 (4)	.5 (8)	.5 (10)	.5 (25)	+ .5
(d) soc. of the family	3.7 (12)	6.8 (36)	6.5 (61)	5.7 (86)	5.3 (102)	5.7 (297)	+ 1.6

Social Change and Economic Development has held a position of importance in Indian sociology and the number of studies has increased especially in the past fifteen years (Table 7). The sub-category of market structures and consumer behaviour has decreased slightly and the type of research being conducted has changed. In the earlier time periods research was directed towards analyses of cooperatives for banking, marketing agricultural products and related functions.[42] Recent studies in market structure and consumer behaviour still have shown some tendencies towards the study of cooperatives but in addition new types of research are present to include consumption patterns and mass marketing within the Indian context of a developing economy.[43]

The sub-category of social change and economic development has increased 2.8% since 1947-1952. Studies in the earliest period emphasized economic development and the role of government planning in achieving this development, for example through the First Five-Year Plan.[44] In later years, however, there has been more emphasis on the changes in society that economic development has produced, for example, how industrialization and urbanization have effected values, patterns of change in village life, the impact of modernization on tribal groups and the impact of economic and social changes on the caste system.[45]

Attention has been directed towards barriers to change, especially in rural areas and towards traditions that have continuity in one form or another in spite of modernization.[46] The role of government as a body for directing change has been investigated as well as India's development in relation to the rest of the world and the westernization of some aspects of Indian society such as M.N. Srinivas's chapter on "Westernization" in *Social Change in Modern India*.[47] Researchers into social change have made some attempts in establishing approaches to studying social change and economic development considering different values in eastern and western societies.[18] This field has also shown a tendency towards more interest in theoretical frameworks than other areas, for example theories of the stages of economic growth and those of social change.[49] As of late, from 1968 to 1972, there appears to be a few researchers that are becoming alarmed by the rapidity and effects of economic development and social change. They use words such as crisis and dilemma in Indian society indicating that there is great concern over problems that economic and social

TABLE 7

Subject Category and Sub-categories	1947-52	1953-57	1958-62	1963-67	1968-72	1947-72	% Change 1947-52 to 1968-72
V Social Change and Eco. Dev.	4.9 (16)	4.9 (26)	5.5 (52)	6.2 (83)	7.5 (143)	6.3 (331)	+ 2.6
(a) soc. change and eco. dev.	4.3 (14)	4.9 (26)	5.3 (50)	5.5 (83)	7.1 (135)	5.9 (308)	+ 2.8
(b) market struc. and consumer	.6 (2)	—	.2 (2)	.7 (11)	.4 (8)	.4 (23)	— .2

TABLE 8

Subject Category and Sub-categories	1947-52	1953-57	1958-62	1963-67	1968-72	1947-72	% Change 1947-52 to 1968-72
VI Demography and Human Biology	1.8	7.4	8.5	5.6	5.2	6.0	+ 3.4
	(6)	(39)	(80)	(83)	(99)	(307)	
(a) demography	1.5	5.5	6.3	3.5	3.0	3.9	+ 1.5
	(5)	(29)	(59)	(52)	(57)	(202)	
(b) human biology	—	—	—	.1	.1	.1	+ .1
				(1)	(2)	(3)	
(3) family planning	.3	1.9	2.2	2.0	2.1	2.0	+ 1.7
	(1)	(10)	(21)	(30)	(40)	(102)	

transformation have produced.[50] This concern might lead to a greater number of studies in this field which are more problem-oriented in that a particular problem is analysed and this explanation or diagnosis provides relevant information for government planners who need to make decisions as to how problems will be solved.

The category of Demography and Human Biology has grown substantially since 1952. Increases have come from the growth of family planning research and demographic studies (Table 8). Family planning research has grown in response to the government's implementation of the official family planning programme in 1952. From its beginning family planning research has studied national programmes and the role of government in this area. Valuable research has been conducted into the characteristic attitudes of adopters and non-adopters in terms of social and economic factors and into social and cultural barriers to family planning.[51] Other researchers have discussed communication between husbands and wives as a factor in the acceptance or rejection of family planning, cultural factors which aid in the implementation of family planning and the sociological implications of family planning.[52]

Since 1947 demographers in India have faced the problem of an over-populated country. Research has been conducted into the rates of birth, fertility, infant mortality, death and migration and attempts have been made to determine factors responsible for these rates.[53] Comparative studies have been conducted between different groups with the population and between different regions in India.[54] The composition of India's population has been noted as it changes through time and recently attempts have been made at formulating population projections from existing data.[55] Population migrations within India have constituted an area of research in terms of the movement of different occupational groups and the rural-urban movement.[56] Population trends have been examined in the light of India's food supply and their relationship to the standard of living and economic development.[57] In more recent years researchers have considered problems of data collection and the validity of population statistics from some sources.[58] Awareness has also developed as to the role of the demographer and social scientist in India considering the population problem.[59]

S. Chandrasekhar has published an encompassing work entitled *Infant Mortality, Population Growth and Family Planning In India.*[60]

Chandrasekhar has made an outstanding contribution to Indian demography but this recent publication is of special note in that it synthesizes many aspects of Indian demography that had previously not been related to one another in such a comprehensive manner. His analysis also includes policy recommendations. Several demographers engaged in Indian sociological research are oriented toward problems of population growth.

Mass Phenomena ranked seventh in amount of research conducted over the past twenty-five years (Table 9). Research into the sub-category of communications is especially important. Research into communications is dominated by studies on the adoption and diffusion of innovations, which are primarily agricultural improvements for rural areas. Characteristics of adopters and non-adopters have been determined as well as channels through which information that influences decision-making to accept or reject will flow.[61] The diffusion of innovations and their adoption has been discussed within a theoretical framework perhaps more so than other subject areas. There is also more use of quantitative techniques, thus theories are at times mathematical models.[62] To a much lesser extent research has been conducted into the effectiveness of mass media such as newspapers, movies and radios.[63] Research in this sub-category appears to serve an evaluative role for government programmes for agricultural improvement and as a source of data which the government could use to plan more effective programmes. (The sudden increase in studies from 1958-62 to 1963-67 is probably the result of a bias introduced into the body of data by taking entries from a book[63a] that provided an intensive bibliography of literature on communications and innovations from the middle 1960's. Excluding this bias, research in communications appears to rise steadily in number throughout the twenty-five year period.)

Other sub-categories under mass Phenomena have changed less dramatically than communications. Social movements has decreased by 10%. In the first two periods research in this area mainly centred on cooperative movements and the rise of Indian nationalism, as would be expected considering India had just gained Independence.[64] In later years the emphasis shifts to studies of the Bhoodan-Gramdan Movement and other movements for social reform and change.[65] The sub-category of public opinion has grown only slightly. Entries in this field are mainly concerned with

TABLE 9

Subject Category and Sub-categories	1947-52	1953-57	1958-62	1963-67	1968-72	1947-72	% Change 1947-52 to 1968-72
VII Mass Phenomena	3.7 (12)	3.3 (18)	4.4 (42)	8.8 (131)	5.5 (94)	5.8 (307)	+ 1.3
(a) social movements	2.2 (7)	.9 (5)	.5 (5)	.5 (7)	1.2 (22)	.9 (46)	− 1.0
(b) public opinion	—	.9 (5)	—	.2 (3)	.2 (4)	.2 (12)	+ .2
(c) communication	1.5 (5)	1.3 (7)	3.4 (32)	8.0 (120)	4.0 (76)	4.6 (240)	+ 2.5
(d) collective behaviour	—	—	.2 (2)	—	—	.0 (2)	.0
(e) sociology of leisure	—	.2 (1)	.3 (3)	.1 (1)	.1 (2)	.1 (7)	+ .1

TABLE 10

Subject Category and Sub-categories	1947-52	1953-57	1958-62	1963-67	1968-72	1947-72	% Change 1947-52 to 1968-72
VIII Political Interactions	8.0 (26)	4.0 (21)	3.1 (29)	5.6 (85)	5.7 (110)	5.2 (272)	— 2.3
(a) interactions between societies, nation, states	.6 (2)	.6 (3)	—	.5 (8)	.2 (4)	.3 (17)	— .4
(b) political sociology	7.4 (24)	3.4 (18)	3.1 (29)	5.1 (77)	5.5 (106)	4.9 (255)	— 1.9

the determining of attitudes among Indian society, for example, about border clashes and education, plus some research into the influence the press has had on government and society.[66] Collective behaviour and the sociology of leisure are two new fields that appear to be at a standstill. Perhaps problems encountered in Western industrialized societies as to the form of activity chosen to occupy leisure time has not yet appeared in India.

The category of Political Interactions has declined since 1947-52 by 2.3% (Table 10). This decline appears mainly because of the interest in political processes generated by India's independence. Interest was also expressed at this time as to the effect British rule had had on India.[67] Once this initial interest in the politics of independence had ended, studies into political interactions dropped in number and then gradually began to increase again in the early sixties. More recent studies in political sociology are concerned with the working of the institution of panchayati raj and local self-government.[68] Investigations have been made into voting trends and behaviour, factionalism in the village setting, the relationship of political process of social change, the interplay of caste and politics and the working of democracy in India.[69]

Research concerned with the interaction between societies and states has decreased slightly. Studies in this sub-category deal with India's relations with neighbours such as Pakistan, Ceylon and China and more distant countries such as the United States. Included in this category also are studies into the work of organizations such as UNESCO and the Ford Foundation in India and research into India's international image.

Research into Social Problems and Social Welfare has increased 2.4% in the past twenty-five years (Table 11). The greatest increase has come from research activity in the sub-category of social disorganization and crime. Studies in this sub-category include those which deal with social tensions and conflict produced by inter-group relationships. A number of such studies were compiled and in some cases, written by L.P. Vidyarthi and published in *Conflict, Tension and Cultural Trend in India*.[70] Crimes of a particular type have received attention as well as analyses of crime from the viewpoint of particular groups in society, for example as in R. Ahiya's work entitled *Female Offenders in India*[71] and C.B. Mamoria's article entitled *The Criminal Tribes in India*.[72] Crime has been approached also from the point of view of environmental factors as well as the relationship of crime to Hindu values.[73]   In more recent years a number of works have appeared dealing with the problems of suicide and social alienation.

Applied sociology or social work has also grown in number of studies. Social work research has concerned itself with analysis of services provided for women and children and particular groups of people, for example occupational groups such as labourers and rehabilitation programmes for tribal groups. Research has been conducted into the formation and role of voluntary associations, the idea and implications of a welfare state in India and the administration and coordination of social services. The concept of social work in India has been examined in the light of traditional Indian thought such as that expressed in the Gita or the philosophy of Karma Yoga notably by G.R. Banerjee.[74] Different approaches to social work have been put forward, such as the Gandhian approach, and problems have been investigated as to conflicting value systems and particular social work approaches.[75] Social work education and training has also received attention, for example, as to the value of American training.[76]

Two new fields of research have come into being, which are social gerontology and delinquency. From the field of social gerontology it appears that older people in India are another aspect of the social change wrought by the transition of a traditional society to one that is modern. Sociological studies of the aged examine the problems they face of declining authority and socio-economic security. Another recent avenue of research has been on delinquency. Most entries in the category deal with juvenile offenders and their reformation. Attempts have been made to explain delinquency considering many factors related to group sentiments, emotional state, socio-economic environment and family life.

The sub-category of works that are general or consider social problems broadly has declined slightly. From the growth of new sub-categories it appears that there is a trend towards approaching problems in a more specialized manner instead of one researcher attempting to investigate them all. Social problems in India have become complex phenomena that require indepth analyses for explanation in terms of the many factors which cause them.

The category of Complex Organizations has increased slightly since 1947-52 (Table 12) and is of considerable importance in Indian

TABLE 11

Subject Category and Sub-categories	1947-52	1953-57	1958-62	1963-67	1968-72	1947-72	% Change 1947-52 to 1968-72
IX Social Problems and Social Welfare	3.3 (11)	4.2 (22)	6.0 (57)	3.9 (58)	5.7 (110)	4.9 (259)	+ 2.4
(a) social problems	.3 (1)	.2 (1)	.2 (2)	.1 (2)	.2 (4)	.2 (10)	— .1
(b) social gerontology	—	—	.2 (2)	.1 (1)	.2 (4)	.1 (7)	+ .2
(c) social dis-organization	1.5 (5)	1.5 (8)	1.3 (12)	1.0 (15)	2.5 (48)	1.7 (88)	+ 1.0
(d) applied soc. (s.w.)	1.5 (5)	2.3 (12)	3.5 (33)	2.2 (33)	2.2 (42)	2.4 (126)	+ .7
(e) delinquency	—	.2 (1)	.8 (8)	.5 (7)	.6 (12)	.5 (28)	+ .6

TABLE 12

Subject Category and Sub-categories	1947-52	1953-57	1958-62	1963-67	1968-72	1947-72	% Change 1947-52 to 1968-72
X Complex Organizations	4.3 (14)	7.3 (38)	4.8 (45)	3.9 (59)	4.9 (93)	4.8 (253)	+ .6
(a) industrial sociology	4.0 (13)	6.5 (34)	4.6 (43)	3.7 (56)	3.7 (70)	4.2 (217)	— .3
(b) military sociology	—	—	—	—	.4 (7)	.1 (7)	+ .4
(c) bureaucratic structures	.3 (1)	.8 (4)	.2 (2)	.2 (3)	.8 (16)	.5 (27)	+ .5

sociological research. The increase of .6% has been the result of the addition of a new category, military sociology and the growth of research in bureaucratic structures. Research in military sociology, according to this analysis, has appeared only after 1968. The majority of research is centred on problems the caste system produces in the military, attitudes of students towards compulsory military training and the military's role in nation building. Stephen P. Cohen has especially contributed to this sub-category, for example in his book *Indian Army : Its Contribution to the Development of a Nation*[77] and his articles "The Untouchable Soldier" "Caste, Politics" and "The Indian Army."[78]

The sub-category of bureaucratic structures has grown slightly since 1952. In earlier periods most research on bureaucracies was done into public and government administration. In later years the study of bureaucratic structures in India continued to concentrate on government and public structures, although new forms of research were also undertaken. For example, studies were conducted that examined levels of socio-economic development and bureaucracy[78] and the implementation of economic plans and bureaucracy.[79] Research has also been conducted of the bureaucracy at different levels of government such as at the district level. Some interest has been expressed in the field of human relations within bureaucratic structures, for example, patterns of authority and subordination in organizations[80] and the orientation of workers towards the norms of bureaucracy.[81] It would seem that as India becomes more developed, the study of bureaucratic structures will continue. Considering the development that has already taken place, both in the public and private sectors it is perhaps surprising that so little research is present in this subject area.

Industrial sociology has decreased in relative frequency by 3% since 1947-52. Earlier studies in industrial sociology, approximately pre-1953, are mostly socio-economic surveys of labourers in particular industries or which examine living conditions and the evolution and composition of groups of labourers. Trade unions, labour welfare and labour reform are also subjects of research in earlier years.[82] These topical emphases and approaches continue in later years but beginning in the middle 1950's until the present, the number of studies dealing with human relations within industrial complexes increases. Research has been directed towards problems such as employee morale and motivation,[83] conflicts in industry, employee communication and consultation, labour and personnel management, collective bargaining and labour participation in management.[84] Particular groups of people in industry have been the object of study such as the conditions and problems of women workers[85] and the effects of caste within industrial organization.[86] Sociological aspects of productivity have received some attention in the light of production planning[87] and social conditions of workers.[88] Very recently some researches have been conducted into the phenomena of strikes.

The category of Social Psychology is shown as declining by 1.4% (Table 13). This decline is caused by a large decrease in the sub-category of attitudes, sentiments and motives. The large number of studies in this sub-category in the first time period is probably due to the inclusion of chapters as separate entries from one edited book on group prejudices in India.[89] As a result the amount of research in this area in subsequent time periods appears to be decreasing when, in fact, after 1952 it is steadily increasing. There is also a slight decline in the sub-category for general works in social psychology. These appear to be mainly works of the text-book variety. In later time periods some attempt is made to discuss general principles of social psychology in reference to the Indian context.[90]

The studies in the sub-category of attitudes, sentiments and motives in the first two time periods covering 1947 to 1957 are concerned with group prejudices in India and attitudes before and after Independence.[91] Some research was also done into the world view of a tribal group. The effects of Independence and the state of India again are felt within the realms of sociology where a new nation attempts unification and as a result scientific investigations begin into the problems of group prejudices in society, religion and politics and its sociological background. In the late 1950's more attention was directed towards the effects foreign elements have had on Indian minds, for example India's attitude towards China.[92]

In more recent time periods, approximately 1963 to 1972, research has been more inclined towards studying how attitudes, values and norms are effected by forces of modernization in Indian society. There has also been interest in the changing attitudes of working women and attitudes towards them of other segments of society.[93] Examination of the effects of encounters with foreign elements continue. Only new questions have been asked such as

TABLE 13

Subject Category and Sub-categories	1947-52	1953-57	1958-62	1963-67	1968-72	1947-72	% Change 1947-52 to 1968-72
XI Social Psychology	5.8 (19)	2.2 (11)	3.1 (30)	3.3 (49)	4.4 (86)	3.7 (195)	— 1.4
(a) general social psy.	.3 (1)	.2 (1)	.1 (1)	.1 (2)	—	.1 (5)	— .3
(b) attitudes, sentiments etc.	4.6 (15)	.4 (1)	.6 (6)	.3 (4)	.8 (16)	.8 (43)	— 3.8
(c) interactions within small groups	—	—	.2 (2)	.3 (4)	.1 (2)	.2 (8)	+ .1
(d) personality and culture	.6 (2)	.8 (4)	.8 (8)	.9 (14)	1.0 (20)	.9 (48)	+ .4
(e) leadership	.3 (1)	.8 (4)	1.4 (13)	1.7 (25)	2.5 (48)	1.7 (91)	+ 2.2

inquiry into how westerners are affected by living in India[94] and the attitudes students abroad have towards returning to their country of origin in the light of the loss of professional skills.[95] Group prejudices have been examined from the viewpoint of perception of prejudice by particular groups, for example caste groups and the effect of inter-caste relations on attitudes.[96] A small amount of research has taken place into the world view of a group of industrial workers.

A new field of research is present after 1957 that are interactions within small groups or group dynamics. Studies in this sub-category have examined factors responsible for group productivity, competition and cooperation in groups, social interaction within villages, factionalism and group interaction patterns of municipal councils.

Studies in personality and culture have grown in relative frequency by .4% since the first time period. In earlier periods research was conducted into basic personality in traditional Hindu culture and problems of the effects of social cataclysm and cultural contact on personality.[97] In more recent years the field has changed towards a greater emphasis on personality changes that have resulted from modernization. Problems of women such as role conflicts caused by social change have also been examined.[98] Some work has also been done in the determination of personality types of particular groups such as castes and tribes and comparisons have been made between these groups in regard to aspects such as intelligence and self-perception.[99] The formation of values has been related to personality structure and in the case of modern values orientations, to style of life.[100] National stereotypes and provincial stereotypes in India have been delineated.[101] Research has progressed in the realm of personality and culture in light of community development, for example, the impact of community development on personality,[102] and attitudes of the personality adjustment of village level workers.[103]

Beginning approximately in 1958 and continuing into the sixties more research is evident into the application of western tools and techniques in the Indian context. For example, research was conducted to determine the validity of particular intelligence tests, tests of self-concepts and socialization scales in India. The majority of research that has been completed in this area has been the product of American scholars or Indians working with Americans and publishing in the United States.[104]

Studies in leadership have grown by 2.2% since 1947-52 and essentially constitute a new avenue of research. Leadership was first examined in the 1950's with regard to identification of leaders in villages with some emphasis being placed on changes in village leadership patterns.[105] In later years the identification of village leaders was still common but more research was directed towards the dynamics of leadership or changes.[106] Recently, leadership has also been examined in settings other than the village such as in trade unions, business organizations, government and political parties and among students.[107] More detailed analyses into leadership have been conducted, for example, into types of leadership and measurement of leadership by reputation or by action.[108] Leadership has been related to development programmes in the light of the impact community development has had on rural leadership and the role of leaders, both elected and opinion, have in the communication of agricultural practices.[109] Recent interest has also been expressed into famous Indian leaders such as Nehru and Gandhi and into traditional Indian concepts of leadership.

The Sociology of Education in India immediately after Independence is characterized by many reports of government organizations. This appears to be a time when previous education programmes were being evaluated, the present situation was being determined and new plans were being made. Reports appear at this time on tribal education,[110] social-education,[111] adult education,[112] primary education,[113] university education[114] and educational reforms.[115] There is also evidence of a trend where attempts are made to integrate traditional aspects of Indian life into education : for example, by examining the role of folk music and folk dance in education and another examination of particular trends in the Indian philosophy of education.[116]

In later periods the Sociology of Education began to increase in relative frequency. Studies were conducted into the progress of education in India, especially for tribal groups, and into the effects of education,[117] factors retarding education and criticism of educational programmes.[118] In the late sixties several new problems within the sociology of education receive more attention than they had previously. Research has been conducted into the social background of different groups of students such as female students.[119] Problems related to eductional institutions and their functioning have been examined, for example the problems of university reform and the task of education administration.[120] More research has been directed towards the effects of higher education on students, such as M. Cormack's *She Who Rides A Peacock*[121] in contrast to the former emphasis on the basic education of tribal groups and rural inhabitants. There appear studies on university students' unrest and politics,[122] the problems of students abroad and student alienation.[123] The impact of education on scheduled castes and tribes and other groups has been examined in the light of social change as well as the effects other variables have on the education of students such as teachers' job satisfaction, rural-urban residence and caste grouping.

Community development has increased by 3.4% in relative frequency since 1952. The lack of studies prior to 1952 is explained by the fact that community development was not put into wide practice in India until that time. Community development research in India was characterized in the 1950's by studies that examined community development in rural areas. Generally, a microcosmic or case study approach was used to investigate community development on communities and community development's relationship to economic growth were assessed. Work was also carried out on the mechanics of community development in the form of guides to community development, the training of community development personnel and local leaders and the process of evaluation of community development projects. Attempts were also made to point out areas where knowledge that was needed for the implementation of community development projects was lacking, for example, the need for knowledge of group structure in villages.

Although research into rural projects continued, at the beginning of the 1960's there is evidence of more research into aspects of urban community development. Interest at this time in urban community development corresponds to the implementation of urban community development in India. The Delhi Pilot Project has been researched intensively by many scholars such as by M.B. Clinard in his book entitled *Slums and Community Development*.[124] Research into the administration of community development programmes also became more prevalent. Subjects investigated were organizational strains, planning interministerial cooperation, institution building and supervision in community development. Aspects of training community development workers were also being examined in the light of new results from projects as to the most effective way to carry out community development. In the mid 1960's research was concerned with the future of community development and in experimenting with new approaches and unconventional ideas. Recently, since 1968 more precisely, more interest has been expressed into the extent of citizen participation in community development and the roles personnel within the community development organizational structure assume and their relationships. This indicates closer attention to the principles of community development, or the theory which underlies community development, in contrast to former research which has had partially by necessity, a very practical orientation.

Urban Sociology has fluctuated in relative frequency but essentially has returned to the relative number of studies in 1947-52. The peak of 4.8% in 1958-62 is due partially to the inclusion of chapters as separate entries from an edited book on urban India published in 1962.[125] The high number of studies in 1947-52 are mainly socio-economic surveys of larger cities in India such as Poona and Hyderabad and a few which examine new towns in India also primarily using the socio-economic framework.[126]

In later years during the 1950's more studies were conducted using an ecological approach.[127] The ecological approach sought to answer questions that socio-economic surveys had omitted, for example, the relationship between cities and their hinterlands and spatial distributions within the city. In respect to these problems contributions to urban sociology in India were made by geographers whose approach of considering regions topographically, economically and socially led to valuable insights as to the relationship between urban physical structure. Another aspect of urban sociology in India that appeared at this time was the study of the persistence of rural settlement types within urban areas and the village-like character of many neighbourhoods in Indian cities.

During the 1960's the socio-economic approach and the ecological approach continued to be used by urban sociologists working in India. These kinds of studies however took on new dimensions and focused attention on particular aspects of urban life such as ethnic or religious communities within metropolitan areas, urban living and working conditions, social structure in planned cities and patterns of residence by education, income and occupation. There has been much more concern expressed over the dynamics of urban life, for example the impact of urbanization on former rural residents, kinship and modernization in the urban context, and systems of communication among urban dwellers. Urban centres and urbanization have also been examined in their relationship to economic development, industrialization and regional planning. The data provided by these studies as well as that from socio-economic surveys and ecological studies have provided valuable information for development and city planning. Within the most recent time period there are many more studies than previously conducted which deal with problems in urban society such as slums, unrest and a lack of integration and communication because of the presence of regional cultures.

Within the category of Sociology: History and Theory, all sub-categories have increased (Table 14). The sub-category of professional interest consists of publications that concern sociologists but do not really belong to other subject areas. Early entries in the sub-category are generally popular works that describe some aspects of Indian life that are of interest to sociologists. In the late 1950's and onward more research was undertaken as to the role of the social sciences in the development of India. The period from approximately 1962 to 1972 was marked by more examinations of problems encountered in social science research and different approaches to the study of societal problems. The teaching of social sciences in India has also received attention considering progress that has been made and problems that must be resolved. In the last time period more investigation has been present into the effects of nationalism on the social sciences and the politics of social research.

The sub-category of history and the present state of sociology includes publications that are essentially opinions of the paths sociology in India has taken, problems and related aspects of its present state and speculations over changes researchers believe would be beneficial in the future. The number of such entries has increased since 1947-52. In the earlier time periods research in this sub-category was concerned with establishing and surveying the status and role of sociology after Independence and its relationship to the other social sciences. More recent trends have been characterized by a greater emphasis on discussions between sociologists over the "best" approach, method and techniques one could adapt to study Indian society and to a lesser extent over the theoretical

TABLE 14

Subject Category and Sub-categories	1947-52	1953-57	1958-62	1963-67	1968-72	1947-72	% Change 1947-52 to 1968-72
XV Sociology : History and Theory	1.8 (6)	2.8 (15)	3.1 (30)	2.9 (42)	3.7 (70)	3.1 (164)	+ 1.9
(a) of professional interest	.6 (2)	.2 (1)	.7 (7)	.7 (10)	.7 (13)	.6 (33)	+ .1
(b) history and present state of soc.	.6 (2)	1.5 (8)	1.7 (16)	1.3 (19)	1.4 (27)	1.4 (72)	+ .8
(c) theories, ideas and systems	.6 (2)	1.1 (6)	.7 (7)	.9 (13)	1.6 (30)	1.1 (59)	+ 1.0

assumptions that underlie their studies. Reference can especially be made here to the articles of this nature that have appeared in *Contributions to Indian Sociology*.[128] Some attention has also been directed towards political and ethical constraints on Indian sociologists and towards the problem of academic colonialism.

The sub-category of theories, ideas and systems has increased in relative frequency since 1947-52 by 1%. Earlier studies were very broad in scope dealing with theories and ideas that applied to all of society. In later years, approximately beginning in the early 1960's, more inquiry ensued on the place of theory within the social sciences. Theories and ideas during the last three time periods generally were trying to integrate aspects of traditional Indian thought into social concepts and social theories, for example the concept of ritual in modern social theory and social concepts in the Hindu value system. There is some evidence that mathematical tools are being used to aid in model building, for example, there was one publication on a cybernetic model of total Indian society in 1967.[129] Interest has also been expressed in the social philosophy of famous and influential Indians such as Nehru.

One of the greatest relative declines in subject area has been in the Sociology of Religion. From approximately 1947 to 1957 studies in the sociology of religion addressed themselves mainly to topics that do not examine religion within the context of modern Indian society. Research into religious and religio-magic practices, rites, deities, mystics and folk religion have been prevalent.[130] There has also been a trend in which religious beliefs were examined through their depiction in ancient literature and texts such as the Epics.[131] Interest was expressed in Christianity within the Indian context and the social relationships between Christians and Hindus and Moslems. In regard to different religious groups in India some work was done in the field of religious prejudices in India and their effect on natural unity. With few exceptions little research was conducted at this time into the changes religious practices were undergoing or into the less stable aspects of religious life.

Research in the sociology of religion beginning roughly in the late 1950's attempted to examine new questions and topics in Indian religion and its relationship to society. Sociological studies were completed which examined the life of priests and temples and their function within communities. Religion was studied in the role it played within society, for example as a means of social control and its relationship to traditional attitudes. The place of religion in society was also examined in regard to nationalism in India and the problem of national integration. Some investigations attempted to reach conclusions about the origin and development of religious movement. New emphasis was also placed on changing religious practices in Indian society.

Although new avenues of research were pursued in the sociology of religion, former trends were still present. The interest in Christianity in India was expressed in studies that related to the impact of Christianity on villages, the problems of groups of Christians and encounters between Christianity and Hinduism. Likewise studies of the religious life, practices, ceremonies and deities of particular groups received considerable attention with the addition of new studies of ideas such as the concepts of pure and impure and the forms of communication within religion. Aspects of traditional Indian thought have remained a focus of study, for example studies in continuities of Indian religious thought and fatalism in Hindu and Islamic thought.[132]

Very recent trends in the sociology of religion in India would indicate that more research is concerned with changes in religious thought and the relationship between economic and social change and religion. C.P. and Z.K. Loomis have examined this relationship intensively in *Socio Economic Change and the Religious Factor in India*.[133] Work has been done to determine the degree of religious change Indian society has undergone, the networks of religion and economics within Hindu thought and industrialization and religious organizations. New approaches have been taken towards the study of interaction between different religious groups in India, for example, a study by S. S. Anant "Stereotypes of Hindus about different religious groups of India" (*Man in India*, 52:2,1972, pp. 123-131) examined stereotypes held by Hindus about different groups.

Group interactions has declined in relative frequency by 1.8% since 1947-52. The decline seems to be present because of the initial high number and then after this peak, the category begins to increase slowly in relative position. The initial high relative frequency of research was due to an interest immediately after Independence in factors that influenced national unity such as Hindu-Moslem relations. The resultant minority groups and refugees from partition of the Indian subcontinent into two sovereign states, India and Pakistan produced problems in Indian society that required investigation.

Once this initial interest in problems of Indian unity and refugees and minorities subsided in the 1950's more research appeared on group dynamics within the village setting and among tribal groups. This avenue of research continued into later years when emphases was placed on the problems of integrating tribal groups and delineating social interaction within multi-ethnic communities and between tribes. The problem of national unity has continued to be of interest and has been approached from the viewpoint of identifying unity within Indian diversity and the effects of regionalism on unity. Refugees and migrant groups have been studied, in some cases examining the social conditions and degree of integration of people displaced in the late 1940's. Research has also been conducted into the nature of communities in border areas. Minorities within India have received much more attention in recent years, for example, the Anglo-Indians and other foreign elements within the Hindu population. Many studies in this category since the early 1960's have dealt with Indian communities overseas and their problems for example in Burma, Fiji, Africa and the United Kingdom.

The Sociology of Medicine in the first ten years was dominated by studies of tribal medicine. For example, some articles were published on tribal medicine men and the folklore of diseases where illness is believed to be caused by certain gods and demons. Such studies generally took a social and cultural anthropological approach as they were conducted by anthropologists, for example Verrier Elwin.[134] During the later 1950's these studies began to be replaced by investigations into social aspects of disease causation and control. Studies in aspects of folk medicine have not completely vanished but in more recent years folk medicine has been examined to a greater extent in light of the impact of modern medicine and technology.

The sociology of medicine during the 1960's included studies primarily on the social and cultural factors affecting health and nutrition and those factors acting as either barriers or aids to the acceptance of new health practices and programmes. Studies have also been undertaken of health among urban dwellers and industrial workers. Particular groups of afflicted people within Indian society have been researched, for example the blind and

TABLE 15

Subject Category and Sub-categories	1947-52	1953-57	1958-62	1963-67	1968-72	1947-72	% Change 1947-52 to 1968-72
XVIII Sociology of Health and Medicine	.6	2.9	1.9	1.7	1.6	1.7	+ 1.0
	(2)	(15)	(18)	(25)	(29)	(89)	
(a) sociology of medicine	.6	2.7	1.6	1.5	1.3	1.5	+ .7
	(2)	(14)	(15)	(22)	(24)	(77)	
(b) social psychiatry	—	.2	.3	.2	.3	.2	+ .3
		(1)	(3)	(3)	(5)	(12)	

TABLE 16

Subject Category and Sub-categories	1947-52	1953-57	1958-62	1963-67	1968-72	1947-72	% Change 1947-52 to 1968-72
XIX Social Control	1.5 (5)	.8 (4)	1.5 (14)	1.3 (19)	1.7 (23)	1.5 (75)	+ .2
(a) sociology of law	1.5 (5)	.6 (3)	1.3 (12)	1.0 (15)	.8 (16)	1.0 (51)	— .7
(b) penology and correctional problems	—	.2 (1)	.2 (2)	.3 (4)	.9 (17)	.5 (24)	+ .9

lepers, in regard to their problems, social conditions and adjustment to disease and handicaps. Within the past five years more research than before has taken place into aspects of social organization and structure within hospitals.

Social Control is another subject area which experienced a greater relative frequency in the period 1947-52 than in later years and then gradually began to increase in proportion to approximately the same level in the final time period (Table 16). The initial peak is due to interest immediately after Independence in the Indian Constitution and in new legislation such as the Hindu Code Bill. These legal documents have been studied in regard to their development, social background and possible modernizing effects, for example, legal recognition of equal rights of women.

Since the 1950's and especially in the last ten years much work has been done into the role of lawyers in Indian society, relationships among lawyers and the changing social origins of lawyers. Social legislation has been studied broadly and in reference to particular groups such as women, children and backward classes. Research has also been conducted in the realm of specific aspects of social legislation such as matrimony. Similarly, law has been examined from the point of view of police in a welfare state, labour and judiciary in India and the British administration of Hindu law. Another trend in the sub-category of the sociology of law has been the study of the modernization of law and the displacement of traditional law and the role of law as an instrument in social change. M. Galanter has made a notable contribution to the Sociology of Law in India, his works covering many of the above-mentioned topics.[135] The impact of social legislation on rural communities and on social control has recently received attention.

The sub-category of penology and correctional problems constitutes a new subject area since 1953 and has grown by .9%. In India, penology and correctional problems has concerned itself with aspects of the probation system and the effects of different kinds of institutionalization on prisoners, for example short-term imprisonment and the effect of prison industries in the rehabilitation of discharged prisoners. Recently, in the last time period, a greater amount of research has been directed towards the administration of prisons, different aspects of prison guards and police within a developing society.

TABLE 17

Subject Category and Sub-categories	1947-52	1953-57	1958-62	1963-67	1968-72	1947-72	% Change 1947-52 to 1968-72
XX Sociology of the Arts	2.7 (9)	1.5 (8)	1.2 (11)	1.3 (20)	1.2 (22)	1.4 (71)	—1.5
(a) soc. of lit. and language	1.5 (5)	1.1 (6)	1.0 (9)	1.2 (18)	.9 (17)	1.1 (56)	—.6
(b) soc. of art	1.2 (4)	.4 (2)	.2 (2)	.1 (2)	.3 (5)	.3 (15)	—.9

Declines in both the sociology of language and literature and the sociology of art constitute the 1.5% relative decline in the category Sociology of the Arts. The sociology of language and literature was dominated until 1958 by publications on the folklore and folk literature of different areas in India and different tribal groups.[136] Interest was also prevalent in the kinship terminology of particular groups in India.[137] During the later three time periods the sociology of language and literature has continued to contain works on kinship vocabulary. Folk literature and traditional Indian literature has received considerable attention especially in the analysis of recurring ideas and trends within this literature. One study examined the creation of a particular Jain story and its parallel Hindu story[138] and another has compared oral versions of literature to the written versions.[139]

A new trend has been a growing interest in the Indian novel, for example, its birth and development, its translation into English and main thematic trends. Research has progressed in the field of linguistic variations because of such aspects as social stratification and the subsequent dialect differences among castes. Another recent trend had been in the form of a greater number of studies concerned with linguistic problems in India and national development and integration. To a less extent research has been conducted into the language of specific groups, for example, the underworld in West Bengal[140] and students' attitudes toward the use of English.[141]

The sociology of art has not changed very much in topical emphases of publications. From the beginning point of this analyses until 1972 much interest has been shown in tribal art and dancing and in traditional Indian music and dancing and their social bearing. Art has been examined in its social context in the form of the social background and folk origins of Indian art and the manner in which art has depicted ancient social life. Art in India has also been examined in its role in society and its social implications, for example the social implications of tribal arts, the social value of art, and art and ritual as methods of social control and planning. The social thought of modern day asthetics has been investigated. In more recent years some work has been completed on the development of handicrafts in India and the handicrafts board.

TABLE 18

Subject Category and Sub-categories	1947-52	1953-57	1958-62	1963-67	1968-73	1947-72	% Change 1947-52 to 1968-72
XXI Methodology and Research Technology	1.2 (4)	.6 (3)	2.1 (20)	1.5 (22)	1.3 (24)	1.3 (73)	+ .1
(a) methodology	.6 (2)	.4 (2)	.6 (6)	.7 (10)	.4 (8)	.5 (28)	— .2
(b) research technology	.6 (2)	.2 (1)	1.2 (11)	.6 (9)	.8 (15)	.7 (38)	+ .2
(c) statistical methods	—	—	.3 (3)	.2 (3)	.1 (1)	.1 (7)	+ .1

Methodology and Research Technology has remained a relatively small field of research in India. In regard to publications in the sub-category of methodology very few changes are present in publication topics since 1947 (Table 18). The methodology of various specialized branches of sociology has been discussed, for example in the study of tribal cultures, caste, group structure, rural and urban society and political values. Various methods, such as comparative approaches, interactionist and holistic small scale studies, have been examined as to their applications, limitations and value. The interdisciplinary method of research has likewise been of interest to sociologists working in India.[142]   General works on the methodology of the social sciences and training in the methods of the social sciences have also been published, for example by S. Dasgupta[143] and N.A. Thoothi.[144]

Research technology has increased slightly since 1947-52, however, it does not appear that any very marked changes have taken place in emphasis or problems researched. Throughout the twenty-five year period there appears to be a greater emphasis on research tools such as field methods and techniques and data collection techniques for social and cultural anthropologists. Another sizeable proportion of work has been done in the examination of survey techniques in India. Questions have been asked pertaining to the applicability of survey techniques, limitations of survey data, urban and rural surveys, family planning surveys and other problems related to this method of data collection. Other data collection techniques and field techniques have been the object of a smaller amount of research.[145]   Contributions to this subject area have also come from social psychologists who have done research into the measurement of specific psychological factors in phenomena such as stereotypes, social attitudes and personality. Some work has also progressed into the realm of scaling techniques for caste ranking and field techniques for studying rural leadership. More recently, approximately in the last ten years some publications have appeared that deal with research procedures in general within the context of a developing society and problems of social research in India.

The sub-category of statistical methods has only come into being after 1958 and does not appear to be growing very rapidly or even moderately. Some work has been done into the methods and problems of sample surveys and the collection of statistical data.

To a lesser extent the use of specific statistical tools has been examined such as probability models and Mahalanobis's D^2.[146] Also research has been published on general statistical methods for the social sciences and the use of statistics in the social sciences.

The category of Planning and Forecasting has declined slightly since 1947-52. The majority of planning research in the first two time periods was concerned with planning to meet the needs and tackle problems which faced the newly formed Indian government such as population pressures, economic development and social change. In later time periods new problems were the foci of interest for example in the areas of planning for technological change in agriculture, educational programmes, urban growth and targets for family planning. More interest has been expressed in the social impact of planning measures taken by the government and in India's basic planning machinery. Planning has been examined considering new ideas such as socio-economic models for planning[147] and the concept of planning rural growth centers for integrated area development.[148]

The Sociology of Knowledge has increased slightly in relative frequency but still constitutes only a very small amount of research in Indian sociology (Table 19). The nature of publications does not appear to change very much through time. There has been a recurring theme of examining the traditional sources of Indian thought within the framework of the sociology of knowledge. Particular groups within Indian society have been studied from the perspective of the sociology of knowledge, for example myth and reality about private enterprise in India, extent of rational thoughts in educated India, regional elites in a theory of modern Indian history and the impact of economic policies on Indian scientists. In one study humanism was examined from the point of view of western and eastern thought.[149] Different branches of Indian scholarship have been studied in their relationship to factors which have had a bearing in their development such as the British policy towards Indian historical research and publication,[150] and the social sciences as related to the study of Indian economic history.[151]

The history of ideas constitutes a new field in Indian sociological research since 1958. Most of the publications in this sub-category are concerned with the study of traditional Indian. thought. Social philosophy in ancient India has received considerable attention as has the origin and development of social thought

TABLE 19

Subject Category and Sub-categories	1947-52	1953-57	1958-62	1963-67	1968-72	1947-72	% Change 1947-52 to 1968-72
XXIII Sociology of Knowledge	.3 (1)	.2 (1)	.3 (3)	.5 (8)	.6 (10)	.4 (23)	— .3
(a) sociology of knowledge	.3 (1)	.2 (1)	.2 (2)	.4 (6)	.2 (3)	.2 (13)	— .1
(b) history of ideas	—	—	.1 (1)	.1 (2)	.4 (7)	.2 (10)	— .4

in India. Research has been conducted in many cases using ancient literature such as the Epics and traditional sources of information about Manu as in K. Motvani's work, *Manu : The Origins of Social Thought.*[152]

The Sociology of Science has decreased by .2% since 1947-52 and has not been growing in recent years relative to other subject areas. In the earlier time periods research was concerned with examining the place of science in building a united India[153] and with technological change in rural areas. During the 1960's the effects of technology and science on society were the major objects of study. Some research was also conducted into social and cultural barriers to technological change. Within the past five or six years there has been some interest in the process of introducing techno- logy and science into agricultural and traditional civilizations. One researcher hoped to point out lessons that could be learned from the Indian experience and another sought to end the fallacy that technological change and the industrialization of traditional agrarian societies automatically means Westernization or that there is no alternative course of development than that which took place in the West.[154]

Studies in Poverty has come into being as a field of sociological research in India since 1958. The appearance of studies in the category perhaps indicates that sociologists are taking a more specialized approach to social problems. Research in this category from 1958 to 1962 has investigated the problems of beggars in India and their socio-economic conditions. Usually, a microscopic approach was taken of studying beggars in a particular city or region. More recent studies have tended to be broader in scope dealing with the poverty problem throughout the whole of India in relation to the caste system, economic development, politics, birth control, food supply and many other variables.

The category of Environmenal Interactions where interactions between man and his natural environment are examined, constitutes another new field of research. Sociological studies of this kind have attempted to study society in its natural environment and changes which are experienced by that society in relation to the physical world. Such an objective for research is not entirely sociological in nature but, nevertheless, raises important questions which greatly concern man's social life and the view of man taken by social scientists. Studies of this type have examined enironmental determinism and the problem of the discrepancy between the view of man held by the natural sciences and that of the social sciences.[155]

Studies in Violence has commanded very little research attention from Indian sociologists. One study examined conflict from the point of view of Gandhian philosophy and the conquest of violence. Another research was concerned with analyses of communal riots and disturbances in various parts of India.

From the foregoing analysis of trends in different subject areas of sociology during the period 1947-72 it can be concluded that definite shifts have taken place in topical emphases prevalent in Indian sociological research. In order to ensure that frequency changes have not been due to normal sampling fluctuations, the chi-square test was used. Cross tabulations were obtained for each five-year time period and each subject category with the exception of the categories of Environmental Interactions, Studies in Poverty and Studies in Violence. These three categories were omitted because their low frequencies would have statistically invalidated the chi-square value. The chi-square value was calculated to be 299.3 with 92 degrees of freedom and found to be significant at the .005 level. Therefore the hypothesis that there is a relationship between subject classification and time was accepted and the foregoing quantitative presentation can be explained by actual changes in sociological research, not chance variations.

References

1. Aalok, S.W., "The Morang Organization among the Nokte Nagas," *Vanyajati*, 4, 2, 1956, pp. 73-78.
   Gough E. Kathleen, "The Social Structure of a Tanjore Village," in *Village India*, editor M. Marriott, (Chicago: University of Chicago Press, 1955), pp. 36-52.
   Mathur, K.S., "Some Aspects of Social Organization in a Malwa Village," *Agra University Journal of Research*, 3, 1955, pp. 100-108.
   Smith, M.W., "Social Structure in the Punjab," in *India's Villages*, editor M.N. Srinivas, (Bombay: Asia Publishing House, 1956), pp. 144-160.
2. I. Karve, *Kinship Organization in India*, (Poona: Deccan College, 1953), 304 pp.
3. K.M. Kapadia, *Hindu Kinship*, (Bombay: Popular Book Depot, 1947) 320 pp.
4. P. Prabhu, *Hindu Social Organization*, (Bombay: Popular Book Depot, 1954), 393 pp.

5. D.A. Chekki, "Modernization and Kin Network in A Developing Society," India, Paper presented at the 7th World Congress of Sociology, the International Sociological Association, Varna, Bulgaria, Sept. 14-19, 1970.

D'Souza, V.S., "Changes in Social Structure and Changing Roles of Older People in India," *Sociology and Social Research*, 55, 3, April, 1971, pp. 297-304.

S.C. Dube, "Social Structure and Change in Indian Peasant Communities," in *Rural Sociology in India*, editor A.R. Desai, (Bombay: Popular Prakashan, 1969), pp. 201-206.

6. D.A. Chekki, "Naming Patterns and Kinship Cohesiveness," *Indian Sociological Bulletin*, 5, 4, July, 1968, pp. 233-237.

D.A. Chekki, "Measuring Kinship Orientation," *Indian Journal of Social Research*, 11, 1, 1970, pp. 47-50.

K. Ishwaran, 'Kinship and Distance In Rural India." *International Journal of Comparative Sociology*, 6, 1, March, 1965, pp. 81-94.

S. Vatuk, "Reference, Address and Fictive Kinship In Urban North India," *Ethnology*, 8, 3, July, 1969, pp. 255-272.

7. G. Chattopadhyaya, "Some Recent Changes in Tribal and Rural Cultural in Middle Eastern India," Doctoral Dissertation, University of Calcutta, 1960.

M.S.A. Rao, "Changing Patterns of Culture in Malayalam Region," Doctoral Dissertation, University of Bombay, 1953.

Singh, Yogendra, "Chanukhera: Cultural Change in Eastern Uttar Pradesh," in *Change and Continuity in India's Villages*, editor K. Ishwaran, (New York: Columbia University Press, 1970), pp. 241-271.

8. Iravati Karve, "Some Studies in the Making of a Culture Pattern," in *Essays in Antoropology Presented to S.C. Roy*, editor J.P. Mills, (Lucknow, 1948), pp. 206-214.

9. S.K. Chatterji, "The Indian Synthesis, and Racial and Cultural Inter-mixture in India," Presidential Address, All Indian Oriental Conference, 17th Session, 1953, (Ahmedabad: R.C. Parikh, 1953), 56 pp.

K. Motwani, India: *A Conflict of Cultures*, (Bombay: Thacker, 1947), 99 pp.

D.N. Majumdar, "Acculturation among the Hajong of Meghalaya," *Man in India*, 52, 1, 1972, pp. 46-64.

10. Dhir, D.N., "Tribes of the North Western Border of India," read in the Seminar on Tribal Situation In India, Indian Institute of Advanced Study, Simla, 1969.

C. von Furer-Haimendorf, *The Raj Gonds of Adilabad*: *A Peasant Culture of Deccan*, (London: MacMillan and Co., 1948).

G.S. Nepali, *The Newars*: *An Ethno-Sociological Study of A Himalayan Community*, (Bombay: United Asia Publications, 1965).

N. Patnaik, *Caste and Social Change*: *An Anthropological Study of Three Orissa Villages*, (Hyderabad: National Institute of Community Development, 1969).

11. Victor Barnouw, "The Changing Character of a Hindu Festival," *American Anthropologist*, 56, 1, Feb. 1954, pp. 74-85.

K. Gnanamble, "The Magical Rites of Uralis (Agricultural, Puberty, Pregnancy and Curing of Diseases)," *Bulletin of the Department of Anthropology*, 4, 2, 1955.

R.K. Gulati, "Pongal: A Deeply Tradition-Oriented Festival of The South," *Journal of Social Research*, 11, 2, Sept. 1968, pp. 150-154.

R.S. and S.A. Freed, "Unity In Diversity In the Celebration of Cattle-Curing Rites In A North India Village: A Study In the Resolution of Conflict," *American Anthropologist*, 68, 3, June 1966, pp. 673-692.

12. R.P. Gondal, "Changes in Customs and Practices Among Some Lower Agricultural Castes of Kotah State," *Eastern Anthropologist*, 1, 4, 1948, pp. 21-28.

M.C. Goswarni and D.N. Majumdar, "A Study of Social Attitudes Among the Garo," *Man In India*, 48, 1, Jan.-Mar. 1968, pp. 55-70.

R.S. Mann, "Some Problems of Indian Tribes," *Kurukshetra*, 14, 11, Aug. 1966, pp. 22-25.

S.P. Rout, "Socio-Economic Implications of Pus Puni Rituals of the Hill Juang of Keonjhar," *Adivasi*, 8, 1966-67.

13. L.K. Mahapatra, "Cultural Anthropology: A Trend Report," in *A Survey of Research in Sociology and Social Anthropology*, vol. III, ICSSR, (Bombay: Popular Prakashan, 1972), p. 18.

14. Howard Becker and Harry Elmer Barnes, "Sociology in India, China and Japan," in *Social Thought From Lore to Science*, vol. III. (New York: Dover Publications, Inc., 1961), p. 1139.

15. G.S. Ghurye, *Caste and Class In India*, (Bombay: Popular Book Depot, 1950), 246 pp.

16. G.S. Ghurye, *Caste, Class and Occupation*, (Bombay: Popular Book Depot, 1961.

17. A.M. Hocart, *Caste: A Comparative Study*, (London: Methuen and Company 1950), 157 pp.

18. L. Dumont, *Homo Hierarchicus: An Essay on The Caste System*, (Chicago: University of Chicago Press, 1970), 385 pp.

19. J.H. Hutton, *Caste In India: Its Nature, Function and Origins*, (Bombay, London and New York: Oxford University Press, 1st ed. 1946, 2nd ed. 1951, 3rd ed. 1961, 4th ed. 1963, reprint 1969), 315 pp.

20. C. Bougle, *Essays on The Caste System*, (introduction by D.F. Pocock), New York: Cambridge University Press, 1971), 228 pp.

21. M.N. Srinivas, *Caste In Modern India and Other Essays*, (Bombay: Asia Publishing House, 1962).

22. A. Beteille, *Castes, Old and New: Essays In Social Structure and Social Stratification*, (Bombay and New York: Asia Publishing House, 1969), pp. 254.

23. C.A. Hate, *Changing Status of Women in Post-Independence India*, Delhi, 1969.

72 THE SOCIOLOGY OF CONTEMPORARY INDIA

24. N. Gupta, "Changing Status of Woman in Hindu Middle Class Society" Doctoral Dissertation in progress, Agra University, 1969.
25. R.L. Goldstein, *Indian Women in Transition: A Bangalore Case Study*, (Metuchen, New Jersey: Scarecrow Press, 1972).
26. M.S. Luchinsky, "The Life of Women In a Village of North India : A Study of Role and Status," Doctoral Dissertation, Cornell University, 1961-62.
27. H. Lamb, "The Indian Merchant," in *Traditional India; Structure and Change*, editor M. Singer, (Philadelphia; American Folklore Society, 1959), pp. 231-240.
   A.B. Mehta, "A Socio-economic Survey of the Domestic Servant Class in Bombay City," Doctoral Dissertation, University of Bombay, 1960.
   K.N.S. Nambudripad, "A Survey of the Occupational and Employment Structure in Some Villages of Malabar," Doctoral Dissertation, University of Bombay, 1949.
28. K.G. Desai, "A Comparative Study of Motivation of Blue Collar and White Collar Workers," *Indian Journal of Social Work*, 28, 4, Jan. 1968, pp. 379-388.
   S.D. Kapoor, "Some Determinants of Job Satisfaction," *Indian Journal of Social Research*, 8, 1, April 1967, pp. 51-54.
   K.L. Sharma, "Occupational Mobility and Class Structure," *Man in India*, 48, 2, April-June 1968, pp. 106-114.
   P.K. Bhowmick, *Occupational Mobility and Caste Structure in Bengal: Study of Rural Markets*, (Calcutta: Indian Publications, 1969) 98 pp.
29. G.H. Gadbois, "Indian Supreme Court Judges: A Portrait," *Law and Society Review*, 3, 2-3, Nov.-Feb. 1968-69, pp. 317-336.
   S.C. Jain, *Indian Manager: His Social Origin and Career*, (Bombay: Somaiya Publications, 1971), 263 pp.
   K.C. North, "The Indian Council of Ministers: A Study of Origins," in *Leadership and Political Institutions in India*, editors R.L. Park and I. Tinker, (New York: Greenwood Press, 1969), pp. 103-115.
30. M.S. Adiseshiah, *Unemployment of Engineers in India*, Impact of Science on Society, 19, 1, Jan.-Mar. 1969, pp. 63-74.
   I.A., Gilbert, "The Indian Academic Profession: The Origins of a Tradition of Subordination," *Minerva*, X, 3, July 1972, pp. 384-412.
   A. Parthasarthi, "India's Brain Drain and International Norms, International Educational and Cultural Exchange, United States, Advisory Commission on International Educational and Cultural Affairs, 1967.
   E. Shils, "The Academic Profession In India", *Minerva* 7, 3, Spring, 1969, pp. 345-372.
31. S.C. Dube, "A Deccan Village," in *India's Villages*, editor M.N. Srinivas, (Bombay: Asia Publishing House, 1956) pp. 180-191.
   Indian Council of Agricultural Research, *Developing Village India: Studies in Village Problems*, editor V.N. Chatterjee: planned by M.S. Randhawa, (Bombay: Orient Longmans, 1951), 290 pp.
   S.K. Jain, "Indian Experiment In Rural Development: The Etawah Pilot Project," *International Labour Review*, 68, 1953, pp. 393-406.

R. Mukherjee, "Economic Structure and Social Life in Six Villages of Bengal," *American Sociological Review*, 14, June 1949, pp. 415-425.

32. M.F. Abraham, "Social Contours of A South Indian Village," *Inter-discipline*, 3, 3, July 1966, pp. 135-149.

S.S. Chauhan, "Agricultural Production Programmes and Social Change in Uttar Pradesh," Doctoral Dissertation in progress, Agra University, 1969.

D. Ensminger, "Problems of Rural Development, Tasks Before Rural Industries," *Kurukshetra*, 15, 5, Feb. 1967, pp. 2-5.

V. Gomathinayagam, "Rural Social Change: Its Correlation to Caste Ranking Economic Position and Literacy Level," *Indian Journal of Social Research*, 13, 3, Dec. 1972, pp. 224-230.

R.D. Lambert, "The Impact of Urban Society Upon Village Life," in *India's Urban Future*, editor Roy Turner (Berkeley: University of California Press, 1962), pp. 117-141.

33. A.B. Bose, "The Structure and Composition of Rural Families," *Indian Journal of Social Work*, 23, 4, Jan. 1963, pp. 351-358.

V.M. Dandekar and V. Pethe, "Size and Composition of Rural Families," *Artha Vijnana*, 2, 1960, pp. 189-199.

A.A. Khatri, "The Indian Family: An Empirically Derived Analysis of Shifts in Size and Types," *Journal of Marriage and the Family*, 34, 4, Nov. 1972, pp. 725-735.

M.K. Nag, "Family Structure of the Kanikkar and Uralis of Travancore," (Government of India : *Bulletin of the Department of Anthropology*, 1954), 3, 3.

34. V. Chowdhury, "Marriage Customs of the Santals," (Government of India : *Bulletin of the Department of Anthropology*, 1953), 1, pp. 86-112.

R.K. Das, "Marriage and Kinship Among the Kakui Nagas of Manipur," *Man In India*, 52, 3, 1972, pp. 228-235.

N.S. Reddy, "Rites and Customs Associated with Marriage in a North Indian Village," *Eastern Anthropologist*, 1955-56, 9, 2, pp. 78-91, Part I: 9, 3 & 4, pp. 178-190, Part II.

S. Singh, "Marriage Rites of the Sonsi Tribe," *Vanyajati* 8, 3, 1960, pp. 155-162.

35. M. Dasgupta, "Changes in the Joint Family in India," *Man in India*, 45, 4, Oct.—Dec. 1965, pp. 283-288.

A.A. Khatri, "Changing Family and Personality of Hindus—A Few Broad Hypotheses," *Vidya*, 7, 2, Aug., 1965.

M.B. Ginger, "The Indian Joint Family in Modern Industry," in *Structure and Change in Indian Society*, editor M.B. Singer and B.S. Cohn (Chicago: Aldine Publishing Society, 1968), pp. 423-455.

36. M.S. Gore, *Urbanization and Family Change* (New York : Humanities Press, 1968), 273 pp.

37. A.D. Ross. *The Hindu Family in its Urban Setting* (Toronto : University of Toronto Press, 1961), 325 pp.

38. K.M. Kapadia, *Marriage and Family in India* (London, Bombay, et al.: Oxford University Press, 1st ed. 1955, 2nd ed. 1958, 3rd ed. 1966), 3rd ed. 395 pp.

39. K. Anand, "Attitudes of Punjab University Women Students Towards Marriage and Family," *Indian Journal of Social Work*, 26, 1, April 1965, pp. 87-90.

R.L. Goldstein, *Attitudes About Marriage Among College Educated Women*, Paper presented at the 65th Annual Meeting of the American Sociological Association, 1970.

N.D. Rao, "Role Conflict of Employed Mothers in Hyderabad, India," Doctoral Dissertation, Mississipi State University, 1970-71.

40. S.S. Anant, "The Changing Trends in Inter-Caste Marriages in India: An Analysis of Matrimonial Columns in English Language Daily," *Journal of Psychological Research*, 16, 1, 1972, pp. 1-5.

K.G. Basavarajappa, "Changes in Age at Marriage of Females and Their Effect on the Birth Rate in India : A Reply," *Eugenics Quarterly*, 15, 4, Dec. 1968, pp. 293-295.

41. M.S. Das, "A Comparative Study of Inter-Caste Marriage in India and The United States," paper presented at the 7th World Congress of the International Sociological Association, Varna, Bulgaria, 1970.

S.J. Murickan, "Family System in India and the United States : A Cross-Cultural Comparison of Educational Adequacy," Doctoral Dissertation, St. Louis University, 1965-66.

M.A. Straus, and M.M. Vasquez, "Adolescent-Parent Conflict in Bombay and Minneapolis in Relation to Social Class and Personality," Paper presented at the 1969 Annual Meeting of the American Sociological Association, Session 52.

G.A. Theodorson, "Romanticism and Motivation to Marry in the United States, Singapore, Burma and India," *Social Forces*, 44, 1, Sept. 1965, pp. 17-27.

42. M.P. Mathur, "Co-operative Marketing in Uttar Pradesh," Doctoral Dissertation, Agra University, 1949.

S.C. Mehta, "Consumer Co-operation in India," Doctoral Dissertation, University of Rajasthan, 1959.

A.P. Singh, "Co-operative Banks," Doctoral Dissertation, Allahabad University, 1951.

43. N. Bhattacharya and B. Mahalanobis, "Regional Disparities in Household Consumption in India," *Journal of the American Statistical Association* 62, 317, Mar. 1967, pp. 143-161.

S. Dandapani, "Consumption Pattern of Class III Clerical Staff of N.E. Railway Headquarters at Gorakhpur : A Sociological Survey and Analysis, Doctoral Dissertation, University of Gorakhpur, 1967.

S.N. Ghosal and M.D. Sharma, "Mass Marketing Model for a Developing Economy," *Indian Journal of Commerce*, 15, 51, Dec. 1964, Part IV, pp. 293-300.

K. Krishnamurty, "Consumption Function for India : A Micro-Time Series Study," *Indian Economic Journal*, 13, 2, Oct.-Dec. 1965, pp. 217-231.

44. D.R. Gadgil, "Economic Development in India," *India Quarterly*, 8, 2, April-June 1952, pp. 171-205.

M.E. Opler, "Economic, Political and Social Change in a Village of North Central India," *Human Organisation*, 11, 2, 1952, pp. 5-12.

V.K.R.V. Rao, "India's First Five-Year Plan—A Descriptive Analysis," *Pacific Affairs*, 25, March 1952, pp. 3-23.

N.V. Sovani, *India's Recent Economic and Social Development With Special Reference To Possibilities of International Cooperation* (New Delhi : Indian Council of World Affairs, 1950), p. 63.

45. K.P. Chattopadhyaya, "Changing Values and Social Patterns in Caste Societies in West Bengal Villages" in *An International Seminar on Paths to Economic Growth*, editor A. Dutta (Poona : Allied Publishers, 1962).

B.S. Cohn, "Changing Traditions of a Low Caste" in *Traditional India* : *Structure and Change*, editor M. Singer (Philadelphia: The American Folklore Society, 1959), pp. 207-216.

T.C. Das, "Aspects of Tribal Culture Under Modern Impact in Eastern India," in *Anthropology on the March*, editor L.K. Balaratnam (Madras: Social Science Association, 1963), pp. 137-154.

Indra Deva, "Social Change in Asia and Its Impact on Folklore and Folk Culture," in *Conspectus of Indian Society*, editor R. Prasad *et al.* (Agra, 1966), pp. 350-364.

J.W. Elder, "Industrialism in Hindu Society : A Case Study in Social Change," Doctoral Dissertation, Harward University, 1958-59.

T.S. Epstein, *Economic Development and Social Change in South India* (Manchester : Manchester University Press, 1962).

T.M. Fraser, J.R., *Culture and Change in India: The Barpali Experiment* (Boston; University of Massachusetts Press, 1969).

S.K. Kuthiala, "Impact of Factory Production on Traditional Societies: Modernization, Some Alternative Views on India," *British Journal of Sociology*, 22, 2, June 1971, pp. 149-159.

M.N Srinivas, *Social Change in Modern India* (Berkeley and Los Angeles: University of California Press, 1968), 194 pp.

46 R.P. Beech and M.J. Beech, *Bengal : Change and Continuity* (East Lansing, Michigan: Asian Studies Center, Michigan State University, May, 1969), 270 pp.

K.G. Ghurye, *Preservation of Learned Tradition in India* (Bombay: Popular Book Depot, 1950), 70 pp.

K. Ishwaran, editor, *Change and Continuity in India's Villages* (New York and London: Columbia University Press, 1970) 296 pp.

47 M.N. Srinivas, op. cit.

48 M.A. Ayyangar, "Economic Development and Moral Values in India: An Historical Approach," *Journal of Social Research*, 8, 1, Mar. 1965.

A. Dasgupta, "India's Cultural Values and Economic Development: A Comment," *Economic Development and Cultural Change*, 13,1, Oct. 1964, Part 1, pp. 100-102.

S. Dasgupta, *Hindu Ethos and the Challenge of Change* (Calcutta, 1972).

R. Dutta, *Values in Models of Modernization* (Delhi, 1971).

49 V.V. Bhatt, "Some Notes on Two Recent Theories of Stages of Economic Growth," *Indian Economic and Social History Review*, 1, 4, April-June 1964, pp. 183-191.

L.R. Klein, "What Kind of Macro-econom∂tric Model for Developing Economies?" Econometric Annual of the *Indian Economic Journal*, 13, 3, 1965, pp. 313-324.

Daya Krishna, *Consideration Towards A Theory of Social Change* (Bombay: Manaktalas, 1965).

V. Pareek, "A Motivational Paradigm of Development," *Journal of Social Issues*, 24, 2, April 1968, pp. 115-122.

M. Sekhar, *Social Change in India: First Decade of Planning: A Theoretical Analysis* (Poona: Deccan College Post-graduate and Research Institute, 1968).

50   C.P. Bhatnagar, *The Crisis in Indian Society* (International Publications Service, 1972).

51   S.S. Balakrishna and B. Radhalyer, "Characteristics of Adopters of Family Planning Methods in Punjab: A Discriminant Function Approach," *Behavioral Science and Community Development*, 2, 1, Mar. 1968, pp. 14-25.

R. Chandra, "Cultural Barriers to Family Planning among Brahmins of Lucknow, city," Doctoral Dissertation, University of Lucknow, 1969.

P.B. Jorapur, "Progress in Family Planning: A Study of Social and Economic Correlation," *Indian Journal of Social Work*, 32 1, April 1971, pp. 77-81.

W.A. Morrison, "The Relationship of Family Size and Socio-cultural Variables to Attitudes Toward Family Planning in a Village of India," Doctoral Dissertation, University of Connecticut, 1956-57.

S. Verma, "Attitudes of Educated Mothers Towards Family Planning in Agra," Doctoral Dissertation, Agra University, 1970.

52   G. Chandrasekaran, "Cultural Factors Aid the Propagation of Family Planning by the Indian Setting," *Journal of Family Welfare*, 5, 3, 1959, pp. 43-51.

G.C. Hallen, "Sociological Implications of Family Planning," *Social Welfare*, 14, 6, 1967, pp. 5-6 and 27.

T. and S.B. Poffenberger, *Husband-Wife Communication and Motivational Aspects of Population Control in an Indian Village* (New Delhi: Central Family Planning Institute, 1969), 117 pp.

53   S.N. Agarwala, "Social and Cultural Factors Affecting Fertility in India." *Population Review*, 8, 1, Jan. 1964, pp. 73-78.

C. Chandrasekaran and M.V. George, "Mechanisms Underlying The Differences in Fertility Patterns of Bengalee Women From Three Socio-Economic Groups," *Milbank Memorial Fund Quarterly*, 40, 1, Jan., 1962, pp. 59-89.

I.Z. Husain, "Educational Status and Differential Fertility in India," *Social Biology*, 17, 2, June 1970, pp. 132-139.

T.J. Samuel, "Social Factors Affecting Fertility in India," *Eugenics Review*, 57, 1, Mar. 1965, pp. 5-14.

54   E. D. Driver, *Differential Fertility in Central India* (Princeton New Jersey: Princeton University Press, 1963), 152 pp.

P.B. Jorapur, "A Comparative Picture of the Demographic Characteristics of Working and Non-Working Women," *Indian Journal of Social Work*, 29, 2, July 1968, pp. 183-192.

G.S. Gosal, "The Regionalism of Sex Composition of India's Population," *Rural Sociology*, 26, 2, June, 1961, pp. 122-137.

W.C. Robinson, "Urban-Rural Differences in Indian Fertility," *Population Studies*, 14, 3, Mar. 1961, pp. 218-234.

55. P.C. Bansil, "The Future Population of India," *Indian Journal of Agricultural Economics*, 13, 3, Jul.-Sept. 1958, pp. 25-43.

C. Chandrasekaran, "Indian Demographic Trends with A Projection into the Next Twenty-Five Years and Their Significance for Social Welfare", *Indian Journal of Social Work*, 26, 2, July 1965, pp. 126-128.

56. N. Mahalingam, "India's Population Problem and Internal Migration," *Population Review*, 8, 2, July 1964, pp. 45-49.

C.R. Prasada Rao, "Rural-Urban Migration: A Clue to Rural-Urban Relations in India," *Indian Journal of Social Work*, 30, 4, Jan. 1970, pp. 335-342.

G.N. Ramu, "Migration, Acculturation and Social Mobility Among the Untouchable Gold Miners in South India: A Case Study," *Human Organisation*, 30, 2, Summer 1971, pp. 170-178.

57. S. Chandrasekhar, "Population Growth and Economic Development in India," *Population Review*, 5, 1, Jan. 1961, pp. 22-26.

K. Krishnamurty, "Economic Development and Population Growth in Low Income Countries: An Empirical Study for India," *Economic Development and Cultural Change*, 15, 1, Oct. 1966, pp. 70-75.

S.P. Malhotra, L.P. Bharara, F.C. Patroa, "Population Resources and Food Situation in Various Tracts within the Arid Zone of Rajasthan," *Indian Sociological Bulletin*, 6, 4, July 1969, pp. 213-221.

W.F. Ogburn, "The Birth-Rate and the Level of Living in India," *Sociologist*, 1, 1, 1956-57, pp. 10-14.

58. S.N. Agarwala, "Age at Marriage in India as Ascertained from Census Data," Doctoral Dissertation, Princeton University, 1957-58.

S.N. Agarwala, "A Method for Correcting Reported Ages and Marriage Durations," *Indian Population Bulletin*, 1, 1, April 1960, pp. 129-164.

S. Chandrasekhar, "A Note on Demographic Statistics in India," *Population Review*, 4, 1, Jan. 1960, pp. 40-45.

59. D.C. Dubey, "Indian Sociology and the Population Problem," *Indian Sociological Bulletin*, 5, 4, July 1968, pp. 209-214.

J.G. Reitz, "Use of Research in Population Programs," Paper presented at the 67th Annual Meeting of the American Sociological Association.

60. S. Chandrasekhar, *Infant Mortality, Population Growth and Family Planning in India* (Chapel Hill, North Carolina: The University of North Carolina Press, 1973), 400 pp.

61. K.L. Bhowmik, P. Das and S. Chatterjee, "Adoption of a Health Variable and Socio-Cultural Characteristics of A Muslim Population in a Rural Region of West Bengal," *Society and Culture*, Special Number, 1970, pp. 23-32.

A.B. Bose, "The Structure of Communication in Different Social Strata in Urban Uttar Pradesh," Doctoral Dissertation, University of Lucknow, 1969.

S.P. Bose, "Characteristics of Farmers who Adopt Agricultural Practices in Indian Villages, *Rural Sociology*, 26, 2, June 1961, pp. 138-145.

S.P. Bose, "The Diffusion of a Farm Practice in Indian Villages," *Rural Sociology*, 29, 1, March 1964, pp. 53-66.

P.C. Deb, "Differential Characteristics of Adopters and Non-Adopters of an Improved Practice," *Indian Sociological Bulletin*, 5, 4, July 1968, pp. 243-247.

M. Satyanarayana, ''An Analysis of Channels of Communication in the Adoption of Some Improved Agricultural Practices in an A.P. Village,'' in *Research Studies in Extension Education* (India, 1966).

62. A.K. Chakrabarti, "A Dissonance Theory Approach to Communication Channel Usage," *Indian Journal of Social Research*, 13, 2, August 1972, pp. 98-110.

F.C. Fliegal and G.S. Sekhon, "Balance Theory and the Diffusion of Innovations, An Empirical Test," Paper presented at the 1969 Meeting of the Rural Sociological Society, Session 42.

63. P.K. Dey, "Relative Effectiveness of Radio and Television as Mass Communication Media in Dissemination of Agricultural Information," Doctoral Dissertation, Indian Agricultural Research Institute, 1968.

J.M. Kapoor and P. Roy, "Role of Mass Media and Interpersonal Communication in the Diffusion of a News Event in India," unpublished paper, Michigan State University, 1969.

Paul Neurath, *Radio Farm, Forum as a Tool of Change in Indian Villages, Economic Development and Cultural Change*, 1962.

M.V. Rao, "The Role of Television as a Medium of Mass Communication, Doctoral Dissertation," University of Poona, 1969.

63a. Rogers, E.M. & Shoemaker, F.F., *Communication of Innovations*, New York, The Free Press, 1971.

64. A.R. Desai, *Social Background of Indian Nationalism* (Bombay: Oxford University Press, 1948), 416 pp.

E.M. Hough, *Cooperative Movement in India* (London: Oxford University Press, 1953), 435 pp.

K.N. Naik, *The Cooperative Movement in Bombay State* (Bombay: Popular Book Depot, 1953), 282 pp.

T.W. Wallbank, *India: A Survey of the Heritage and Growth of Indian Nationalism* (New York: H. Holt, 1949), 118 pp.

65. W. Ekka, "Reform Movements Among the Nagesia," *Man in India*, 52, 2, 1972, pp. 174-182.

L.K. Mahapatra, "Social Movements Among Tribes in Eastern India with Special Reference to Orissa—A Preliminary Analysis," *Sociologus*, 18, 1, 1968, pp. 46-62.

T.K. Oommen, "Charismatic Movements and Social Change: Analysis of Bhoodan-Gramdan Movement in India," Doctoral Dissertation, University of Poona, 1969.

G.N. Ostergaard and M. Currell, *The Gentle Anarchists: A Study of the Leaders of the Sarvodaya Movement for Non-Violent Revolution in India* (New York: Clarendon Press, 1971), 421 pp.

66. S. Agarwal, "The Influence of the Press on the Government and Public Opinion in India from 1900 to 1935," Doctoral Dissertation, Allahabad University, 1956.

A.H. Cantril, Jr., "The Indian Perception of the Sino-Indian Border Clash," *Public Opinion Quarterly*, 28, 2, Summer 1964, pp. 233-242.

P. Ramachandran, "Public Opinion on Education," *Indian Journal of Social Work*, 31, 4, Jan. 1971, pp. 355-365.

67. Examples of early publications in Political Interactions: T. Das, "Status of Hyderabad During and After British Rule in India," *American Journal of International Law*, 43, Jan. 1949, pp. 57-72.

P.P. Lakshman, *Congress and the Labour Movement in India* (Allahabad: All India Congress Committee, 1947), 174 pp.

R.L. Park, "Indian Election Results," *Far Eastern Survey*, 12, 1952, pp. 61-70.

N.V. Rajkumar, *Indian Political Parties* (New Delhi: All India Congress Committee, 1948), 139 pp.

68. A.P. Awasthi, "Rural Local Self-Government in Madhya Pradesh under the Janpada Scheme," Doctoral Dissertation, University of Saugar, 1961.

C.M.B. Lalerao, "Some Social, Political and Administrative Consequences of Panchayati Raj," *Asian Survey*, 4, 4, April 1964, pp. 804-811.

R.L. Park, "District Administration and Local Self-Government," in *Leadership and Political Institutions in India*, editors R.L. Park and I. Tinker (New York: Greenwood, 1969), pp. 337-345.

J.S. Yadar, "Group Dynamics and Panchayat Elections in a Punjab Village," *Journal of Social Research*, 11, 2, Sept. 1968. pp. 58-72.

69. F.G. Bailey, *Politics and Social Change: Orissa in 1959* (Berkeley and Los Angeles; University of California Press, 1963).

R. Kothari (editor) *Caste in Indian Politics* (United States: Fernhill, 1972).

K.G. Krishna Murthy and G.L. Rao, "Socio-Economic and Demographic Factors and Voting Behaviour, The Case of Kerala," *Political Science Review*, 8, 2, April-June, 1969, pp. 193-212.

W. McCormack, "Factionalism in a Mysore Village," in *Leadership and Political Institutions in India*, editors R.L. Park and I. Tinker (Oxford University Press, 1960), pp. 438-444.

P.N. Rastogi, "Vectors of Factionalism," *Indian Journal of Social Research*, 7, 3, Dec. 1966, pp. 186-193.

D.B. Rosenthal, "De-urbanization, Elite Displacement and Political Change in India," *Comparative Politics*, 2, 2, Jan. 1970, pp. 169-201.

L.I. Rudolph and S.H. Rudolph, "The Political Role of India's Caste Association, *Pacific Affairs*, 33, 1, Mar. 1960, pp. 5-22.

C.C. Taylor *et al.*, *India's Roots of Democracy*, (Bombay: Orient Longmans, 1965).

70. L.P. Vidyarthi (editor), *Conflict, Tension and Cultural Trend in India* (Calcutta: Punthi Pustak, 1969), 312 pp.
71. R. Ahuja, *Female Offenders in India* (Meerut: Meenakshi Prakashan, 1969), 131 pp.
72. C.B. Mamoria, "The Criminal Tribes in India," *AICC Economic Review*, 11, 8, Sept. 1959, pp. 19-23.
73. Y.S. Mehendale, "Crime and Environment," *Indian Journal of Social Work* 16, 3, Dec. 1955, pp. 146-152.

S. Pundir, "Slum Culture and Criminal Behaviour," Doctoral dissertation in progress, Agra University, 1969.

A.M. Rose, "Hindu Values and Indian Social Problems," *Sociological Quarterly*, 8, 3 (Summer), 1967, pp. 329-339.
74. G.R. Banerjee, "Karma Yoga and Social Case Work Practice in India", *Indian Journal of Social Work*, 24, 4, Jan. 1964, pp. 229-234.

G.R. Banerjee, "Concepts of Social Work in the Gita," *Indian Journal of Social Work*, 25, 1, April 1964, pp. 29-34.
75. S. Dasgupta, "Gandhian Concept of Non-Violence and Its Relevance Today to Professional Social Work," *Indian Journal of Social Work*, 29, 2, July 1968, pp. 113-122.

K.D. Gangrade, "Conflicting Value System and Social Case Work," *Indian Journal of Social Work*, 24, 4, Jan. 1964, pp. 247-256.

K.D. Gangrade, "Family Centered Approach and Social Case Work," *Indian Journal of Social Work*, 29, 3, Oct. 1968, pp. 277-288.

K.V. Mukundrao, "The Bhagavad-Gita: A Study of its Value Content with Reference to Social Work in India," Doctoral Dissertation, University of Pennsylvania, 1963-64.
76. M.R. Maurya, "Field Work Training in Social Work," *Indian Journal of Social Work*, 23, 1, April 1962, pp. 9-14.

H. Nagpaul, "Dilemmas of Social Work Education in India," *Indian Journal of Social Work*, 28, 3, Oct. 1967, pp. 269-284.

B. Schlesinger, "American Training For Indian Social Worker: Cure or Curse?" *Indian Journal of Social Work*, 21, 3, Dec. 1960, pp. 261-265.
77. S.P. Cohen, *Indian Army: Its Contribution to the Development of a Nation*, (Berkeley and Los Angeles: University of California Press, 1971).

S.P. Cohen, "The Untouchable Soldier: Caste, Politics, and the Indian Army," *Journal of Asian Studies*, 28, 3, May 1969, pp. 453-468.
78. P.K.B. Nayar, "Bureaucracy and Socio-Economic Development; A Case Study of Planning Departments in Two Indian States," Doctoral Dissertation, University of Pittsburgh, 1967-68.
79. H.C. Rieger, "Bureaucracy and the Implementation of Economic Plans in India," *Indian Journal of Public Administration*, 13, 1, Jan.-Mar. 1967, pp. 32-42.
80. S. Kakar, "Authority Patterns and Subordinate Behaviour in Indian Organizations," *Administrative Science Quarterly*, 16, 3, Sept. 1971, pp. 298-307.

81. S.K. Goyal, "Bureaucracy: A Sociological Study of Levels of Orientation of Clerks towards the Norms of Bureaucracy," *Indian Sociological
Bulletin*, 5, 4, July 1968, pp. 248-257.

82. Examples of early research in Industrial Sociology: K.S. Basu, "Philoso-
phies of Labour Welfare," *Indian Journal of Social Work*, 14, 1, June
1953, pp. 58-59.

R.M. Birjay, "Textile Labour in Bombay City: Its Evolution and
Composition: 1934-1949," *Indian Journal of Social Work*, 14, 2, Sept.
1953, pp. 168-177.

S.B. Chirde, "Industrial Labour in Bombay: A Socio-Economic Analysis,
with Special Reference to Industrial Workers residing in Bombay
Development Department Chawls, Bombay," Doctoral Dissertation.
University of Bombay, 1949.

S. D. Punekar, *Trade Unionism in India* (Bombay : New Book Co., 1948),
407 pp.

83. D.M. Pestonjee, "A Study of Employee's Morale and Job Satisfaction
as related to various types of Organizational Structure," Doctoral
Dissertation, Aligarh Muslim University, 1967.

84. T.N. Kapoor, *Personnel Management and Industrial Relations in India*
(Bombay : N.M. Tripathi, 1968), 287 pp.

P.S.K. Murthy, "A Sociological Study of Worker's Participation in the
Joint Consultation Scheme of Indian Industries," Doctoral Dissertation
Duke University, 1959-60.

T.S. Papola, "The Place of Collective Bargaining in Industrial Relations
Policy in India," *Journal of Industrial Relations*, 10, 1, March 1968, pp.
25-33.

V.P. Shintre, "A Study of Communication between Management and
Employees," *Indian Journal of Social Work*, 28, 3, Oct. 1967, pp. 329-334.

85. S.V. Jha, "Socio-Economic Conditions of Women Workers in Organized
Industries of Uttar Pradesh," Doctoral Dissertation, Agra University, 1961.

86. V.S. Parthasarathy, "Caste in A South Indian Textile Mill," *Economic
Weekly*, 10, 11, 15 March 1958, pp. 384-389.

87. K. Chowdhry and A.K. Pal, "Production Planning and Organization
Morale," *Human Organization*, 15, 4 (Winter 1957), pp. 11-16.

88. A.K. Rice, "Productivity and Social Organization in an Indian Weaving
Mill," *Human Relations* 8, 4, 1955, pp. 399-428.

89. M.B. Nanavati and C.N. Vakil (editors), *Group Prejudices in India*
(Bombay: Vora, 1951).

90. S.P. Adinarayan, *Social Psychology with Special Reference to Indian
Conditions* (Bombay and New York: Allied Publishers, 1964).

91. S.P. Adinarayan, "Before and After Independence: A Study of Racial and
Communal Attitudes in India," *British Journal of Psychology*, 44, 2, May
1953, pp. 108-115.

92. S. Arora, "Indian Attitudes Toward China," *International Journal*, 14,
1 (winter, 1958-59), pp. 50-59.

93. S.S. Akhtar, D.M. Pestonjee and F. Farooqi, "Attitudes towards Working
Women," *Indian Journal of Social Work*, 30, 1, April 1969, pp. 93-98.

94. L.M.H. Kidder, "Foreign Visitors: A Study of Changes in Selves, Skills and Attitudes of Westerners in India," Doctoral Dissertation, North western University, 1971.

95. M.S. Das, "Effect of Foreign Students' Attitudes Towards Returning to the Country of Origin and the National Loss of Professional Skill," Doctoral Dissertation, Oklahoma State University, 1969-70.

96. S.S. Anant, "Caste Prejudice and its Perception by Harijans," Journal of Social Psychology, 82, 1970, pp. 165-172.

97. U. Guha, "Effect of Social Cataclysm on Personality," Bulletin of the Anthropological Survey of India, 5, 1, 1956, pp. 1-10.
    D. Narain, Hindu Character (Bombay: University of Bombay Press, 1957).
    P.C. Ray, "The Effect of Culture-Contact on the Personality Structure of Two Indian Tribes—The Riang of Tripura and Baiga of M P." Bulletin of the Anthropological Survey of India, 6, 2, 1957, pp. 1-84.
    W.S. Taylor, "Basic Personality in the Orthodox Hindu Culture Patterns," Journal of Abnormal and Social Psychology, 43, Jan. 1948, pp. 3-12.

98. A. Mahajan, "Women's Two Roles: A Study of Role Conflict," Indian Journal of Social Work, 26, 4, Jan. 1966, pp. 377-380.

99. S.S. Anant, Inter-Caste Differences in Personality Patterns as a Function of Socialization," Phylon, 27, 2, Summer, 1966, pp. 145-154.
    S.S. Anant, "Self and Mutual Perception of Salient Personality Traits of Different Caste Groups," Journal of Cross Cultural Psychology, 1, 1970, pp. 41-52.
    R.R.P. Sinha, "A Comparative Study of Tribal and Non-Tribal Intelligence," Doctoral Dissertation, University of Ranchi, 1966.

100. A.L. Srivastava, "Modern Value-Orientation and Styles of Life," Journal of Social Research, 12, 1, March 1969, pp. 47-55.

101. G.S. Sinha and S.P. Sinha, "A Study of National Stereotypes," Indian Journal of Social Work, 27, 2, July 1966, pp. 163-174.

102. P.A. Bhagwatwar, "A Comparative Psychosocial Study of the Impact of Community Development Programme on Personality Dynamics, Attitudes and Social Change in Rural Community in Maharashtra with Special Reference to Mulshi and Purandhar Taluka," Doctoral Dissertation, University of Poona, 1969.

103. M. Roy and D.K. Mazumdar, "Study in some Personality Adjustment Variables of Village Level Workers," Society and Culture, 1, 1, July 1970, pp. 17-24.

104. E.D. Driver, "Self-Conceptions in India and the United States: A Cross-Cultural Validation of the Twenty Statement Test," Sociological Quarterly 10, 3, (Summer 1969), pp. 341-354.
    H.G. Gough and H.S. Sander, "Validation of the CPI Socialization Scale in India," Journal of Abnormal and Social Psychology, 68, 5 1964, pp 544-547.
    R.S. and S.C.S. Master, "A Comparison of Intelligence Tests in Indian Conditions," Indian Journal of Social Work, 20, 2, Sept. 1959, pp. 125-128.

R.N. Singh, "A Study of the Scores on Cattell's Culture Faire Test of Intelligence (Scale 2) in the Indian Background: A Special Reference to Socio-Economic Variable," Doctoral Dissertation, University of Gorakhpur, 1968.

105. A.R. Beals, "Change in the the Leadership of a Mysore Village," in *India's Villages*, editor M.N. Srinivas, (Bombay: Asia Publishing House, 1955).

Government of India, *Leadership and Groups in a South Indian Village* (New Delhi: Planning Commission, Programme Evaluation Organization, 1955), 9, 134 pp.

106. L.C. Gupta, "Changing Pattern of Rural Leadership: A Case Study," *Sociological Bulletin*, 15, 2, Sept. 1966, pp. 27-36.

P.V. John, "Changing Pattern of Leadership in a Village in Madhya Pradesh," *Sociological Bulletin*, 12, 1, March 1963, pp. 32-38.

B.N. Sahay, *Dynamics of Leadership* (New Delhi: Bookhive, 1968).

107. S.M. Mathur, "A Sociological Study of Trade Union Leadership in Rajasthan," Doctoral Dissertation in progress, University of Rajasthan, 1969.

F. Redlich, "Business Leadership : Diverse Origins and Variant Forms" *Economic Development and Cultural Change*, 6, 3, April 1958, pp. 177-190.

I.B. Tandon, "Emerging Patterns of Leadership Among Students in Rohilkhand Division in U.P. (A Socio-Psychological Study)," Doctoral Dissertation in Progress, Agra, 1969.

108. A. Singh, "Reputational Measure of Leadership: A Study of Two Indian Villages," (State College: Mississippi State University, 1964, and "Action Measure of Leadership: A Study of Two Indian Villages," Paper presented at the Rural Sociological Society, San Francisco, 1967.

109. V.R. Gaikwad and G.L. Verma, "Elected Leaders as Key Communicators of agricultural Practices," *Behavioural Sciences and Community Development*, 4, 1, March 1970, pp. 52-62.

B.N. Singh, "The Impact of the Community Development Programme on Rural Leadership," in *Leadership and Political Institutions in India*, editors P. Park and I. Tinker (Oxford University Press, 1960), pp. 358-371.

110. Examples of early research in the Sociology of Education that deal with tribal education.

T.N. Madan, "Education of Tribal India," *Eastern Anthropologist*, 5, 4, 1952, pp. 179-182.

D.S. Nag, "Education for Primitives," *Vanyajati*, 2, 4, 1954, pp. 117-120.

K. Pakrasi, "Some Aspects of Tribal Education," *Vanyajati*, 4, 4, 1956, pp. 127-133.

G. N. Sen, *The Primary Education For Tribals*, Report of the Second Conference for Tribes and Tribal (Sehi), Areas (Delhi: Bharatiya Adimjati Sevak Sangh, 1953).

A. N. Vyas, "Ten Years' Progress of Ashram Education in Orissa," *Vanyajati*, 6, 4, 1958.

111. India (Republic) Ministry of Education, *All India Report of Social Educa-tion, 1947-51*, Delhi (A report on the adult education movement in India up to 1947 is contained in Chapter 1 of the Teacher's Handbook of Social Education published by the Ministry in 1953).

112. B.Q. Singh, "The Communication of Ideas through Adult Education in India" Doctoral Dissertation, University of Bombay, 1957. Also see note 111 above.

113. G. N. Sen, op. cit.

114. India (Dominion) University Education Commission. *Report, December, 1948-August 1949* (Delhi: Manager of Publications, 1949).
    K. R. Srinivasa Iyengar, *A New Deal for our Universities*, (Calcutta: Orient Longmans, 1951), 134pp.

115. Mysore, Committee for Education Reform, *Report* (Bangalore: Government Press, 1953), 500 pp.

116. A. J. Agarkar, "Social Background of Physical Education, with special Reference to the Folk Dances of Maharashtra—Folk Dance and Physical Education," Doctoral Dissertation University of Bombay, 1947.
    K.D. Seth, "Idealistic Trends in Indian Philosophy of Education," Doctoral Dissertation, Allahabad University, 1953.

117. S.K. Ghosh, "Education and Social Change, NEFA," *Journal of Social Research*, 12, 1, March 1969, pp. 27-37.
    T. B. Naik, *Impact of Education on the Bhils*,, (New Delhi: Planning Commission, 1969).
    A. N. Sachchidananda, "Education and Changes In Social Values," *Man in India*, 48, 1 Jan.-March 1968, pp. 71-85.

118. L. R. N. Srivastava, *Some Basic Problems of Tribal Education*, Report of the National Seminar on Tribal Education in India, N.C.E.R.T. (New Delhi, 1967), pp. 77-97.
    M. Zachariah, "Positive Discrimination in Education for India's Scheduled Castes: A Review of the Problems: 1950-1970," *Comparative Education Review*, 16, 1, 1972, pp. 16-29.

119. M. Verma, "Socio-Economic Study of Under-graduate Girl Students," *Indian Journal of Social Work*, 21, 3, Dec. 1960, pp. 283-286.

120. P. G. Altbach "Problems of University Reform in India," *Comparative Education Review*, 16, 2, Jan. 1972.
    G. Wood, "Planning University Reform: An Indian Case Study (Mysore)" *Comparative Education Review*, 16, 2, June 1972.

121. M. L. Cormack, *She Who Rides A Peacock: Indian Students and Social Change; A Research Analysis* (Bombay: Asia Publishing House, 1961).

122. P. G. Altbach, "Student Politics and Higher Education in India," *Daedalus*, 97, 1, Winter 1968, pp. 254-273.
    G. C. Hallen, (Editorial) "Sociology of Student Unrest," *Indian Journal of Social Research*, 7, 2, Aug. 1966, pp. i-iv.
    A. P. Ross, *Student Unrest in India*, (Montreal: McGill-Queen's University Press, 1969), 301 pp.

123. S. L. Doshi, "The Destudentisation of Alienation: A Problem of disturbed Campus," *Journal of Social Research*, 12, 1, March 1969, pp. 67-77,

R. Mehta, *The Western Educated Hindu Woman* (Bombay: Asia Publishing House, 1970).

A. K. Singh, *Indian Students in Britain* (Bombay and New York: Asia Publishing House, 1963).

124. Marshall B. Clinard, *Slums and Community Development: Experiments in Self-Help* (New York: The Free Press, 1966), 395 pp.

125. R. Turner (editor), "India's Urban Future," Seminar on Urbanization in India (Berkeley: University of California Press, 1962).

126. "Examples of early socio-economic surveys in Urban Sociology: D. R. Gadgil," *Poona: A Socio-Economic Survey* (Poona: Gokhale Institute of Politics and Economics, 1945-52, 2 volumes).

S. Kesava Iyengar, *A Socio-Economic Survey of Hyderabad-Secunderabad City Area* (Hyderabad: The Indian Institute of Economics, 1952), 390 pp.

127. Examples of ecological studies in Urban Sociology: A Bopegamage, "Ecological Study of Delhi City," Doctoral Dissertation, University of Bombay, 1957.

N. P. Gist, "The Ecology of Bangalore, India: An East-West Comparison," *Social Forces*, 35, 4, May 1957, pp. 356-365.

128. F. G. Bailey, "For A Sociology of India?" *Contributions To Indian Sociology*, 3, July 1959, pp. 88-101.

L. Dumont and D. Pocock, "For A Sociology of India?" *Contributions To Indian Sociology*, 1, April 1957, pp. 7-22.

L. Dumong and D. Pocock, "For A Sociology of India? A Rejoinder to Dr. Bailey," *Contributions To Indian Sociology*, 4, April 1960, pp. 82-89.

T. N. Madan, "For A Sociology of India: Some Clarifications," *Contributions to Indian Sociology*, 1, 1967, pp. 90-93.

A. K. Saran has also joined in the discussion in "For A Sociology of India," *Eastern Anthropologist*, 15, 1, 1962, pp. 53-68.

129. P. N. Rastoji, *A Cybernetic Model of Total Indian Society: An Introductory Framework*, (Massachusetts Institute of Technology, Mimeographed, 40, 1967).

130. K Gnanamble, "The Kanikkars of Travancore, Their Religious and Magical Practices," India: *Bulletin of the Department of Anthropology*, 3, 2 1954.

131. K. V. Aiyangar Rangaswami, *Some Aspects of the Hindu View of Life According to Dharmasastra*, Baroda Oriental Institute, 1952.

D. P. Vora, "Evolution of Morals in the Epics—The Mahabharata and Ramayana," Doctoral Dissertation, University of Bombay, 1956.

132. Joseph W. Elder, "Fatalism in India: A Comparison Between Hindus and Muslims," *Anthropological Quarterly*, 39, 3, July 1966, pp. 227-243.

133. C. P. and Z. K. Loomis, *SocioEconomic Change and the Religious Factor in India* (New Delhi: Affiliated East-West Press, 1949).

134. Example of some of Verier Elwin's studies in the Sociology of Health and Medicine using an anthropological approach.

V. Elwin, "Tribal Medicine in India," *Statesman*, March 22, 1953.

V. Elwin, "Folklore of Disease; (1) The Demon of Cholera," *Statesman*, April 5, 1953.

135. M. Galanter, "The Uses of Law in Indian Studies," in *Languages and Areas: Studies Presented to George V. Bobrinskoy* (Chicago: University of Chicago; Division of Humanities, 1967), pp. 37-44.

M. Galanter, "Group Membership and Group Preferences in India," *Journal of Asian and African Studies*, 2, 1-2 1967, Jan.-April, pp. 91-124.

M. Galantar, "The Displacement of Traditional Law in Modern India," *Journal of Social Issues*, 24, 4, October 1968, pp. 65-92.

M. Galanter, *The Aborted Restoration of 'Indigenous' Law in India*, Comparative Studies in Society and History, 14, 1, 1972, pp. 53-70.

D. A. Chekki, "Social Legislation and Kinship in India," *Journal of Marriage and the Family*, 31, 1, Feb, 1969, pp. 165-172.

136. S. Sen, "Folklore and Bengali Literature," *Indian Folklore*, 1, 1956, pp. 44-49.

137. T. N, Madan, "Kinship Terms used by the Pandits of Kashmir: A Preliminary Analysis," *Eastern Anthropologist*, 7, 1953.

138. M. Bhattacharjee, "Creation of the Ganga: Jain Story and its Parallel Hindu Story," *Folklore*, 5, 1964.

139. B. E. Beck, "A Comparison of written and oral versions of A Great South Indian Epic," Paper Presented at the 1971 Annual Meeting of The Canadian Sociological and Anthropological Association.

140. C. Malik, *Language of the Underworld of West Bengal* (Calcutta, 1972).

141. S. Bandyopadhyay and A. L. Ross, "The Attitudes to and Use of English by Students of Three Different Mother Tongues, Hindu, Kannada, and Tamil," Paper presented at the South Asia Symposium, Anthropological Seminar, 1970.

142. B. Krishnarao, "The Descriptive Method in Social Research," *Sociological Bulletin*, 10, 2, 1961, pp. 46-52.

L. K. Mahapatra, "The Values and Limitations of Holistic Small Scale Studies," Proceedings and Papers of the Seminar on Research Methodology in the Social Sciences, Indian Institute of Economics, 1967.

R. N. Saksena, *Interdisciplinary Approach in Social Research*, Regional Seminar on Techniques of Research, UNESCO Research Centre, New Delhi, 1959, pp. 141-143.

G. Sarana, "Comparative Methods (Approaches) in Social-Cultural Anthropology: A Methodological Analysis," Doctoral Dissertation, Harvard University, 1966.

H. C. Srivastava, "Radhakamal Mukerjee's Inter Disciplinary Method and Frame of Reference in Social Science," *Indian Journal of Social Research*, 8, 1, April 1967, pp, 33-38.

143. S Dasgupta (editor), *Methodology of Social Science Research*, International Publication Service, 1967.

144. N. A. Thoothi, *Methods of Social Research*, International Publication Service, 1966.

145. K. Srinivasan, "A Probability Model applicable to the Study of Inter-Live Birth Intervals and Random Segments of the Same," *Population Studies*, 21, 1, July 1967, pp. 63-70.

146. R. Mukherjee and S. Bandyopadhyay,"Social Research and Mahalanobis's D," *Contributions to Statistics* (Calcutta, 1963).

147. B. P. Adhikari, "Construction of Socio-Econometric Models for Planning," *Eastern Anthropologist*, 13, 3, March — May 1960, pp, 84-94.

148. L. K. Sen, S. Wanmali, S. Bose, G. K. Misra and K. S. Ramesh, *Planning Rural Growth Centres for Integrated Area Development: A Study of Miryalguda Taluka* (Hyderabad, India: National Institute of Community Development, 1971), 245 pp.

149. R. Mukherjee, "Humanism, East and West," *Indian Journal of Social Research* 7, 3, December 1966, pp. 178-185.

150. J. H. Voight, British Policy Towards Indian Historical Research and Writing, 1870-1930," *Indian Economic and Social History Review*, 3, 2, June 1966, pp. 137-149.

151. T. Raychaudhuri, "The Social Sciences and the Study of Indian Economic History, 1600-1947," *International Social Science Journal*, 17, 4, 1965, pp. 635-643.

152. K. Motwani, *Manu: The Origins of Social Thought* (Bombay: Bhartiya Vidya Bhawan, 1970), 100 pp.

153. S. S. Bhatnagar and S. D. Mahant, "Place of Science in Building of a United India," in *Group Prejudices in India*, editors M. B. Nanavatti and C. N. Vakil (Bombay: Vora, 1951), pp. 219-223.

154. S. K. Kuthiala, "Impact of Factory Production on Traditional Societies: Modernization Some Alternative Views on India," Paper presented at the 7th World Congress of the International Sociological Society, Varna, Bulgaria, 1970.

155. A. K. Saran, "The Natural Sciences and the Study of Man: The Problem of their Synthesis in Contemporary Culture," *Eastern Anthropologist*, 14, 2, 1961, pp. 122-135.

FOUR

Major Patterns in Nationality of Author and Place of Publication

Results from frequency counts of authors' nationality clearly showed particular trends in this aspect of Indian sociological research. The most marked shift has been an increase in the proportion of total research output being the work of Indian authors. The greater number of Indian sociological researchers has been primarily the result of expanding sociology departments in universities and because of government encouragement and funding of research in Indian society. Sociology in Indian universities has grown greatly since 1947. The discipline has acquired an independent position of its own as a branch of study separate from political science, economics and anthropology. It is now taught in over half of India's universities[1] and has proved to be very popular at both the undergraduate and post-graduate levels, attracting quite a large number of students. From data collected for this analysis as to type of publication it was found that the number of dissertations in sociology and some from related disciplines such as social anthropology, economics, political science and social psychology increased from 36 completed dissertations in 1947-52 to 273 completed dissertations in 1968-72 and with 270 still in progress at the time of writing.

The society and social problems of India have not attracted academic interest alone. The government of India since Independence has made efforts to stimulate research in the social sciences and to relate the social sciences to problems of development. Especially since the late 1950's, several specialized social science institutes and centres have been established. Universities and research centres have been financed by state and federal governments in order that studies may be undertaken on development problems and in order to accumulate scientific knowledge on various aspects of Indian society to help the government in the task of transforming a tradition-bound society into one that is modern and fully industrialized.[2]

Expanded university facilities in sociology, encouragement from the Indian government in terms of financing and interest among students in studying the problems facing their society have all helped to increase the number of Indians engaged in sociological research. As these factors have been at work to establish sociology as a professional field in India and to attract more research activity in sociology, the number of scholars from the United Kingdom engaged in sociological research in India has declined sharply. Although it has been stated that Indian sociologists continue to remain attached to the apron strings of British sociology,[3] the evidence here suggests that the British influence is waning. The British influence in Indian sociological research was primarily in the realm of social and cultural anthropology. These fields of research activity have declined greatly in the past twenty-five years. It appears that younger British scholars have not been drawn to India in as great numbers as in former times. This stands to reason as politically India and Britain have separated and as tribal groups modernize and village life changes, the attraction that was present twenty-five or more years ago of studying in a British colony the interesting aspects of an entirely foreign people is no longer there.

As the British influence in Indian sociology declined, it has been replaced, it appears, by American influences. The number of American scholars has increased slightly since 1947-52. It may be assumed that with this foreign element in Indian sociological research and the increasing number of Indian students receiving post-graduate training in the United States, American sociological foundations have had widespread influence in India. The presence of American scholars undertaking research on Indian society could possibly be explained by the increased number of fellowships and grants made available by American foundations and programmes to study in developing countries. Many noteworthy American scholars who have done research in India first were enabled to do so by financial aid from these American funding bodies. American aid in India since Independence has not only been financial. Often technical expertise of professional skills have been sent to help in

TABLE 20

Indian Sociological Research, 1947-1972: Cell Frequencies In per cent and Number and Rank Order (1947-1972) by Nationality of Author

Nationality of Author	1947-52	1953-57	1958-62	1963-67	1968-72	1947-72	% Change 1947-52 to 1968-72
Indian	61.6% (199)	66.6% (351)	70.2% (663)	77.8% (1168)	78.4% (1499)	74.5% (3893)	+ 16.8%
North American	9.9 (32)	16.9 (89)	14.7 (139)	10.1 (152)	10.8 (206)	11.9 (620)	+ .9
Not known	20.1 (65)	11.4 (60)	8.1 (76)	6.7 (101)	7.4 (140)	8.5 (444)	− 12.7
United Kingdom	5.6 (18)	2.3 (12)	2.3 (22)	1.8 (27)	.7 (13)	1.8 (92)	− 4.9
European	1.2 (4)	1.3 (7)	2.5 (24)	1.5 (23)	1.1 (21)	1.5 (79)	− .1

						+
At least one Indian	1.2 (4)	.8 (4)	1.1 (10)	1.7 (26)	1.4 (27)	1.4 (71)	.2
Other	.3 (1)	.2 (1)	.3 (3)	.2 (3)	.3 (5)	.2 (13)	0
European and United Kingdom	—	.6 (3)	.7 (7)	.1 (1)	—	.2 (11)	0
Total	100%	100% 527	100% 944	100% 1501	100% 1911	100% 5226	

studying villages to obtain baseline data, conduct evaluation programmes, and to aid in the organization and implementation of development plans and programmes.

Cases where there has been at least one Indian whose name appeared as a member of a research team (two or more than two authors) was taken to indicate foreign collaboration. This variable has increased slightly since 1947-52 from 4 studies (1.2%) in the first time period to 27 (1.4%) in the last. Foreign collaboration then, dose not appear to be seen as an undesirable development by Indian sociologists. Much more research though has probably been done in the form where foreigners decide the direction and scope of research and Indians are used to collect data and act as interpreters. Although such information has not been quantified here, there are many books by foreign authors which give acknowledgement to Indian sociologists for their help in carrying out these necessary but secondary in importance research activities.

The feelings Indians have towards foreign collaboration and foreigners working alone in their country seem to be mixed. In 1955 a strong cry of disapproval of foreign research activities was heard from six social scientists from Lucknow University who doubted the theoretical validity of modern methods of empirical research imported from the West and who believed American and other foreigners were studying India to obtain information for commercial purposes and military objectives.[4] On the other hand, many prominent Indian sociologists have expressed their approval of foreign collaboration in order that Indians may keep abreast of theoretical developments elsewhere[5] and in order that new insights be gained through the mechanism of seeing oneself through the eyes of a stranger.[6] It might be concluded that Indian scholars realize the importance of foreign collaboration but have learned to apply foreign methods and concepts with caution, to question the conclusions reached by foreigners who do not have the advantage of great familiarity with Indian society and to demand a greater voice in the direction of joint research activities with foreigners.

Examination of the number of authors studying Indian society that are European or classified as others indicates that aside from the American increase no new nationalities have undertaken sociological research in India in any significant numbers. The European-United Kingdom classification was found to consist mainly of studies written jointly by D. Pocock and L. Dumont. The unknown classification was the unfortunate result of lack of information about nationality of some authors. Studies classed as unknown however were usually non-Indians and thus could be taken to indicate unspecified foreign elements within Indian sociological research.

The main subjects researched are as under ;

1. Culture and Social Structure
2. Rural Sociology
3. Social Differentiation
4. The Family and Socialization
5. Mass Phenomena
6. Social Change and Economic Development
7. Demography and Human Biology
8. Social Problems and Social Welfare
9. Complex Organizations
10. Political Interactions
11. Sociology of Education
12. Social Psychology
13. Urban Structures and Ecology
14. Community Development
15. Sociology : History and Theory
16. Sociology of Religion
17. Group Interactions
18. Sociology of Health and Medicine
19. Methodology and Research Technology
20. Social Control
21. Sociology of the Arts
22. Planning, Forecasting and Speculation
*23. Sociology of Knowledge
*24. Sociology of Science

*not included in calculation of chi-square value

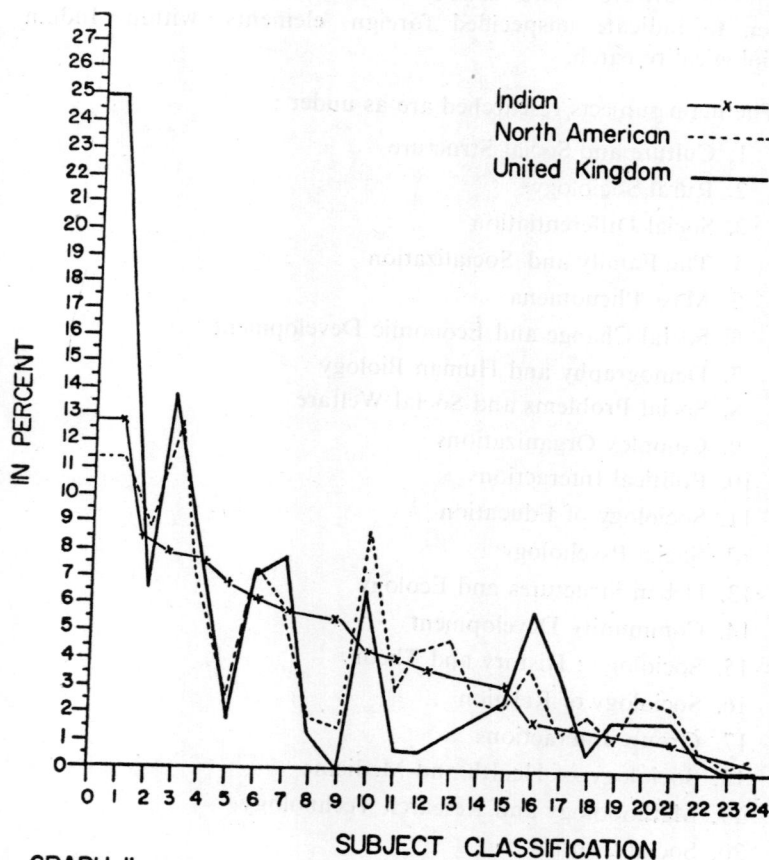

GRAPH II

Indian Sociological Research; 1947-1972: Frequency Distribution of Subject Classification of Research By Indian, North American and United Kingdom Authors.

NATIONALITY AND SUBJECT CLASSIFICATION

To determine if nationality of author was related in any way to subject classification a chi-square test was performed. The relationship between the two variables was found to be significant at the .005 level ($X^2 = 197.5956$ with 42 degrees of freedom). For statistical validity the following variables had to be omitted for nationality of author: European, Other, Not Known, at least one Indian and European-United Kingdom. For subject classification, Sociology of Knowledge, Sociology of Science, Environment Interactions, Studies in Poverty and Studies in Violence were not included.

The cross-tabulations calculated for the chi-square test provided much valuable information in terms of relative and absolute frequencies. Graph II has been produced by graphing subject classification against per cent of research by authors from India, North America and the United Kingdom. A sample reading from the table might be that out of all the research that has been done in the twenty-five years' time period by British authors, 24.9% of it has been in the category of Culture and Social Structure. Subject classifications were placed along the bottom of the graph in rank order from highest to lowest per cent of research in particular subject areas by Indian authors.

The graph is useful in that it depicts the characteristics of the significant relationship between subject classification and author's nationality. Generally, it appears that North American and British authors have tended to emphasize the same subject areas that differ from the topical emphases of Indian authors. However, there still are some wide discrepancies between North American authors and those from the United Kingdom and in their respective degrees of emphasis. There is also some conformity in slope of the three lines, that is, with high frequencies to the left of the graph and gradually tapering to lower frequencies at the right.

British authors have concentrated almost one quarter of their research on Culture and Social Structure, which includes the subcategories of social structure, culture and social anthropology. Emphasis has been placed to a greater extent than that of Indian authors on Social differentiation, Social Change and Economic Development, Demography and Human Biology, Political Interactions, Sociology of Religion, Group Interactions, Methodology and Research Technology, Social Control and Sociology of the

Arts. The majority of research by British authors gives the impression of being concentrated on aspects of Indian society that are alien to British culture such as tribal groups, Indian culture, the caste system, Indian religious systems and Indian arts. British research in the study of Group Interactions has usually been directed towards Indian communities in foreign countries, for example Fiji and Mauritius. The work of British authors in the categories of Social Change and Economic Development and Demography and Human Biology was generally found to have been published after approximately 1960. For the other categories high percentages have been calculated because of the small total frequency of British studies.

British authors have given less attention than Indian authors to Rural Sociology, Mass Phenomena, Social Problems and Social Welfare, Sociology of Education, Social Psychology, Urban Structures and Ecology, Community Development, Sociology of Health and Medicine, Sociology of Knowledge, Sociology of Science and Planning, Forecasting and Speculation. Practical problems of Indian society, then, have not attracted British researchers to any great extent. Research topics that are aimed at examining problems of India in transition have been overlooked, especially in the first two time periods. It may be contended that the research of British social and cultural anthropologists served an administrative purpose but it is mainly during the last fifteen years that India has been studied as an industrializing and modernizing country.

North American authors compared to British authors have conformed to a greater extent to the subject classification distribution of Indian authors, although there are still many differences between the two lines. North Americans have done more research than Indians in Rural Sociology, Social Differentiation, Social Change and Economic Development, Demography and Human Biology, Political Interactions, Sociology of Religion, Social Psychology, Urban Structures and Ecology, Sociology of Health and Medicine, Social Control, Sociology of the Arts, Planning, Forecasting and Speculation and Sociology of Science. Areas that North Americans have de-emphasized are Culture and Social Structure, Mass Phenomena, Social Problems and Social Welfare, Complex Organizations, Sociology of Education, Community Development, Sociology, History and Present State, Group Interactions,

Methodology and Research Technology and Sociology of Knowledge.

North Americans appear to have conformed somewhat to the British in that the more alien, at least, from a Westerner's point of view, aspects of Indian life have been studied. This is shown by a greater percentage of Americans than Indians in Social Differentiation (caste system), Sociology of the Arts and Sociology of Religion. North Americans, though, have also focused attention on contemporary issues in Indian society that Indians have not researched as greatly, such as urban structures, planning and forecasting, sociology of science and technology, political structures, social change and economic development. North Americans have made a contribution to Indian sociology in the form of community studies. Indian sociologists have been criticized for their rural emphasis[7] but in light of the data that has just been shown that foreign authors are no more willing to give up anthropological field studies in isolated villages and move to crowded slums than are Indians. North Americans are shown as directing more attention than Indians to urban structures but still the American rural emphasis is much more dominant than their urban emphasis.

Indian authors have had the highest frequencies in subject areas that are more related to current problems in Indian society as it undergoes the change from tradition to modernity, such as Mass Phenomena (communication of innovations and their adoption), Social Problems and Social Welfare, Complex Organizations (industrial sociology), Sociology of Education and Community Development. It appears that some aspects of Indian society, for example the caste system, are important objects of study for Indian sociologists, but do not hold the same attraction as they do for foreign scholars. It is likely that these aspects of society do not seem to be particularly interesting to Indians who accept them as a part of everyday life. Instead Indians have focused on problems that are more related to India's development.

However, Indians have not fully accepted the challenge their society offers to the sociologists. In this regard, reference is being made to the fact that foreign authors have put more emphasis than Indians on the three important areas: Social Change and Economic Development, Demography and Human Biology, and Political Interactions. It is possible that foreigners have emphasized these areas more than Indians probably because these areas of study are more developed in foreign countries. For example, both the United States and Britain are countries with strong political heritages and their political ideas have been transported to India, in earlier times when India was a British colony, and today when America seems to be interested in the political well-being and stability of developing nations. It is also probable that Americans studying in India have been sponsored by programmes that are aimed at helping developing nations to progress economically and cope with resultant processes of social change.

TRENDS IN PLACE OF PUBLICATION

The cell frequencies from Table 21 for place of publication showed a distinct trend towards more publication of research findings in India and to a lesser extent more publication in North America. This greater increase in amount of publication in India and the United States has been at the expense of publication in the United Kingdom. Several reasons might be postulated for this shift in place of publication. Firstly, the publication facilities in India for sociological research have greatly improved over the past twenty-five years. Not only have national publishing houses and branch offices of foreign publishers expanded but new journals have begun publication such as the *Sociological Bulletin*, the *Indian Sociological Bulletin, Contributions to Indian Sociology* (Old & New Series), *Indian Journal of Social Research, Indian Journal of Sociology* and several others.

With the improvement of conditions in India for the publication of sociological research findings former intellectual ties with the United Kingdom have diminished. Fewer British sociologists and social and cultural anthropologists are engaged in research activities in India. Therefore, as researchers would probably publish in their country of origin, the amount of research being published in Britain has relatively declined. Earlier we have discussed the reasons for the decline in the number of British researchers.

Intellectual ties with Britain have been replaced with a greater degree of academic relationship to North American sociology. North American category was used here to designate studies published in Canada, Mexico and the United States. The vast majority of North American studies had been published in the United States, thus hereafter we shall refer to the United States to

TABLE 21

Indian Sociological Research, 1947-1972: Cell Frequencies in per cent and Number and Rank Order (1947-1972) by Place Of Publication

Place	1947-52	1953-57	1958-62	1963-67	1968-72	1947-72	% Change 1947-52 to 1968-72
India	61.9% (200)	67.6% (356)	65.3% (616)	70.7% (1061)	69.4% (1326)	68.3% (3569)	+ 7.5%
North America	19.2 (62)	20.5 (108)	24.4 (230)	19.1 (286)	22.9 (437)	21.6 (1129)	+ 3.7
Europe	3.7 (12)	4.0 (21)	6.5 (61)	5.5 (83)	4.2 (81)	4.9 (258)	+ .5
United Kingdom	10.5 (34)	5.9 (31)	2.8 (26)	2.5 (37)	1.8 (35)	(3.1) (163)	− 8.7
Not Known	4.0 (13)	2.1 (11)	.8 (8)	1.0 (16)	1.3 (24)	1.5 (76)	− 2.7
Other	.6 (2)	0	.3 (3)	1.2 (18)	.4 (8)	.6 (31)	− .2
Total	100% (323)	100% (527)	100% (944)	100% (1501)	100% (1911)	100% (5226)	

get a clearer picture of where publication activity has taken place. Since India has gained Independence the United States has continued to supply aid and technical expertise to speed the process of economic development and social change. Therefore, as more Americans have been encouraged to study Indian society, more research has been published in the United States, the authors' home base where perhaps there are already established publication channels.

As ties with the United States have grown stronger and because of the academic liveliness of American sociology, more Indian students have found it desirable to study in the United States and in some cases, eventually live there while continuing to publish research findings from their new residences in America. Indians who live in India and have been engaged in sociological research activities may publish in the United States for the prestige that is attached to having their work published by well-known American publishing companies. The United States also offers many opportunities to publish research findings as there are a large number of major well known sociological journals published in the United States.

Research findings have also been published to a slightly greater extent over the past twenty-five years in continental Europe. The majority of works published in Europe have been contained within sociological journals such as the *European Journal of Sociology*, the *International Journal of Comparative Sociology* and *Sociologus* as well as the *Transactions of the World Congress of Sociology* of the International Sociological Association.

To determine whether or not there existed a relationship between subject classification and place of publication the chi-square test was used. Variables for place of publication were India, North America, United Kingdom and Europe. All subject categories were used except Environmental Interactions, Studies in Poverty and Studies in Violence. These omissions were made to meet statistical requirements. The X^2 value was found to be 271.61914 with 69 degrees of freedom, thus the relationship was significant at the .005 level.

The information from cross-tabulations was graphed in the same fashion as nationality and subject classification had been graphed and is presented in Graph III. As would be expected the lines for countries (from Graph III) and their nationalities (from Graph

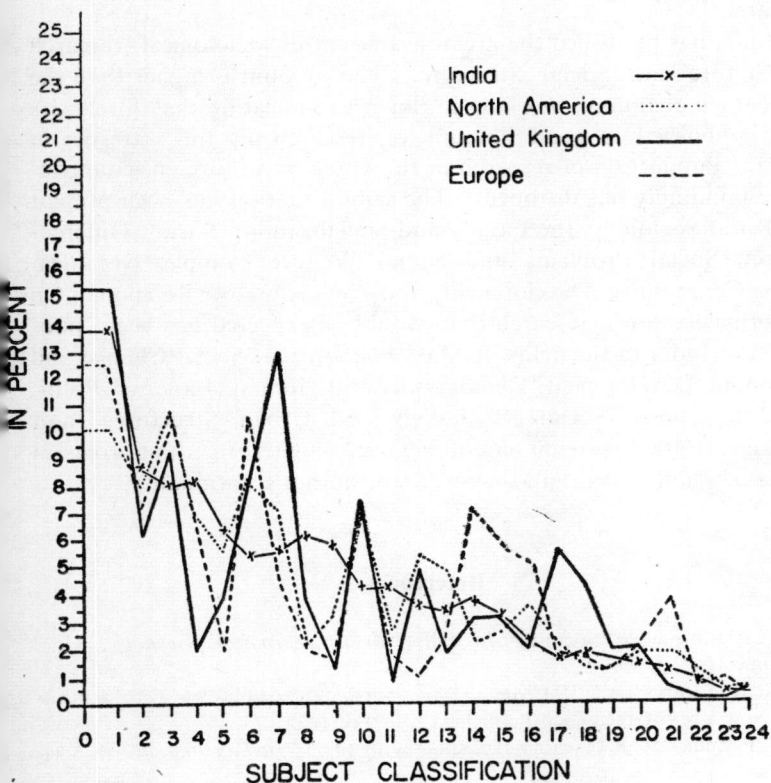

GRAPH III

Indian Sociological Research; 1947 - 72: Frequency Distribution
of Subject Classification of Research Published in India,
North America, the United Kingdom and Europe.

II) correspond quite closely. It must be remembered that percentages do not imply absolute amount of research output. Percentages for Europe and the United Kingdom because of their initial low frequency appear larger than those for India and North America but in actual number represent a much smaller amount of research.

India has published the greatest amount of sociological research in Culture and Social Structure. The amount is higher than the percentage of Indians working in this area indicating that foreigners have published a good amount of research in this category in India. Publication of research in this category in foreign countries correspondingly has dropped. The same situation has been present for Rural Sociology, the Family and Socialization, Social Differentiation, Social Problems and Social Welfare, Complex Organizations, Community Development and Sociology of Religion. On the other hand less research than would be expected has been published in India in the fields of Mass Phenomena, Social Change and Economic Development, Demography and Human Biology, Political Interactions, Social Psychology and Urban Structures and Ecology. Other foreign countries were higher in these areas in place of publication than they were for author's nationality.

References

1. T. B. Bottomore "Sociology In India," *British Journal of Sociology*, 13, 2, June 1962, p. 99.
2. A. K. Saran, "India," *Contemporary Sociology*, edited by J. S. Roucek, (New York: Greenwood Publishers, 1969) p. 1029.
3. J. P. Suda, "The Teaching of Sociology In India," *Indian Journal of Social Research*, 8, 1, 1967, p. 25.
4. A. K. Saran, op cit., p. 1031.
5. I. Ahmad, "Note On Sociology In India," *The American Sociologist*, 1, 5, Nov. 1966, p. 247.
6. M. N. Srinivas, editor, *India's Villages*, (Bombay: Asia Publishing House, 1960), p. 5.
7. M. B. Clinard and J. W. Elder, *Sociology in India: A Study in the Sociology of Knowledge*, American Sociological Review, 30, 4, Aug. 1965, pp. 581-587.

FIVE

Main Trends in Number and Sex of Authors

Indian sociological research has been dominated since the beginning of the study by authors working alone and this trend is continuing. Studies where two authors and three or more authors have collaborated however have also gained in number especially in the last ten years. This would indicate a trend towards more research teams. From Table 20 (on page 90) giving the breakdown of data by author's nationality it is known that in cases where two or more authors have done research and at least one was Indian, constituted 1.4% of total research output for twenty-five years. Out of the 9.5% cases of multiple authorship from Table 22 then, about one-seventh of this research was done by teams of foreigners working with Indians. As from Table 22 the variables measuring two and three or more authors has increased by 5.3%, it can be concluded that research teams are growing in number but that they are mainly made up exclusively of Indians.

An avenue of study which has not been pursued here is the academic affiliations or professional calling of members of research teams. Although this information would be hard to obtain it could be used to measure the amount of interdisciplinary research activities taking place. If nationality of author was included in such an analysis then a picture could be drawn of the nationality of members of inter-disciplinary research teams, answering questions as to who has been receptive to cross-disciplinary study and to what extent Indians as opposed to foreigners and vice versa have taken part in these activities.

The "not known" category was included for the classification of research reports and journal articles that gave no names of specific authors. That this category has decreased does not indicate that

TABLE 22

Indian Sociological Research, 1947-1972: Cell Frequencies in Per cent and Number and Rank Order (1947-1972) by Number of Authors

Number of Authors	1947-52	1953-57	1958-62	1963-67	1968-72	1947-72	% Change 1947-52 to 1968-72
One	86.4% (279)	92.0% (485)	90.3% (852)	86.4% (1297)	87.9% (1679)	88.2% (4609)	+ 1.5%
Two	3.4 (11)	3.6 (19)	6.5 (61)	9.8 (147)	7.4 (141)	7.3 (381)	+ 4.0
Three or more	1.5 (5)	.9 (5)	1.6 (15)	2.5 (37)	2.8 (54)	2.2 (117)	+ 1.3
Not Known	5.9 (19)	2.6 (11)	.1 (1)	.5 (7)	.7 (13)	1.0 (51)	— 5.2
Other	1.2 (4)	.6 (3)	1.4 (13)	.6 (9)	.8 (16)	.9 (45)	— .4
Government Report	1.5 (5)	.8 (4)	.2 (2)	.3 (4)	.4 (8)	.4 (23)	— 1.1
Total	100% (323)	100% (527)	100% (944)	100% (1501)	100% (1911)	100% (5226)	

research reports have declined in number but rather that reports are published to a greater extent in more recent years with specific authors names. In the earliest time period a greater percentage of reports appear with no names indicating perhaps that authors were generally steady employees of research centres. Later the fact that author'(s) names are signed could indicate that individuals conduct research by becoming more or less short-term employees of institutes while they research a particular topic and then leave or begin a new project once they have finished and their grant has expired. It appears to be generally a trend where research reports are the products of individuals working under their own direction instead of where reports are the products of employees assigned to tasks which are directed by research institutes or centers.

The "other" category was included to cover edited books as other author classifications did not apply. A class of government reports also was included for studies done under the auspices of particular departments and ministries and where only the name of the department or ministry was given. This variable or classification for number of authors has declined indicating the decrease in government reports and perhaps the same trend which is taking place in regard to authorship and research reports.

A relationship between number of authors and subject classifications was found by using the chi-square test. The calculated chi-square value was 155.6546 with 40 degrees of freedom. Number of authors was classified as one, two and three or more with the exclusion of the classifications of government reports, others and "not known". All subject categories were used in calculating the chi-square value except Studies in Violence, Studies in Poverty, Environmental Interactions, Sociology of Science, Sociology of Knowledge and Planning, Forecasting and Speculation although cross-tabulations were obtained for these categories. Table 23 lists subject areas that had the most extreme frequencies.

Subject areas that have the highest frequencies for multiple authors are areas of study that usually involve extensive fieldwork over wide areas in the form of interviews and surveys. Examples might be surveys of the acceptance of innovations, health beliefs and practices, community development projects and demographic characteristics of particular populations. Subject areas that have the highest proportions of single authorship to some extent do not have fieldwork as a prerequisite such as Sociology of the Arts and

TABLE 23

Single Authorship ≤ 90%

Subject Category	1 author	2 authors	3 or more authors
Mass Phenomena	77.3%	18.8%	3.9%
Sociology of Health and Medicine	80.7	15.9	3.4
Rural Sociology	85.7	10.3	4.0
Methodology and Research Tech.	85.7	11.4	2.9
Social Psychology	86.4	11.5	2.1
The Family and Socialization	88.3	10.4	1.3
Demography and Human Biology	88.3	9.3	2.3
Community Development	89.0	7.0	4.1

Single Authorship ≥ 95%

Subject Category	1 author	2 authors	3 or more authors
Soc. of Language and Literature	95.7%	4.3%	0%
Sociology of Knowledge	95.7	4.3	0
Group Interactions	95.6	4.4	0
Social Problems and Social Welfare	95.2	3.2	1.6
Complex Organizations	95.1	4.5	.4

Sociology of Knowledge. Group Interactions, Social Problems and Social Welfare and Complex Organizations also are subject areas where fieldwork may not be that important. Research can be based on other sources of Information such as government records, and the approach used is often more qualitative in nature than quantitative. It appears then that the primary reason for subject areas to be particularly high or low in categories of number of authors is because of the different characteristics of each area of study.

SEX OF AUTHOR

The data for sex of author is incomplete because of the amount of studies classed as unknown, especially in the first time period; nevertheless, some conclusions can be drawn. The proportion of male authors has stayed relatively the same for the past twenty years i.e., since 1953 and has declined slightly in the past five years. The proportion of female authors has increased slightly especially in the last five years. Comparing absolute numbers from 1947-52 to 1968-72, the number of male authors has increased itself over six times and the number of female authors has increased over nine times. It appears then that the number and proportion of female authors is growing at a faster rate than male authors especially in more recent years.

Women are slowly beginning to play a more prominent role in Indian sociological research but their contribution is still of minor significance being only 6% of the total research output. An examination of the number of females holding teaching positions in universities and colleges in India in departments of sociology, social work, and social and cultural anthropology from the *Commonwealth Universities Yearbook* for 1972 indicated that 14.6% of the teaching staff was female. Women in Indian sociology therefore have channelled their energy and professional skills into teaching and only under half of this professional group has taken the initiative to conduct research. Teaching at the university level is undoubtedly an important role for women to assume in the development of sociology in India but at the same time valuable skills are not being used and their potential unfulfilled probably because of sex. It is also true that teaching at the university level is usually greatly improved if instructors have had practical experience in researching the particular subject they are teaching. Whatever the barriers to research may be in India for women such as culturally defined roles, it is hoped that in the future, efforts would be made to erase them so that unused skills are tapped and the quality of teaching be improved.

The variable coded as male/female has increased slightly since the first time period. Studies in this class have often been the

TABLE 24

Indian Sociological Research, 1947-1972: Cell Frequencies in per cent and Number and Rank Order (1947-1972) by Sex of Author

Sex of Author	1947-52	1953-57	1958-62	1963-67	1968-72	1947-72	% Change 1947-52 to 1968-72
Male	72.8% (235)	78.4% (413)	77.0% (727)	79.6% (1195)	77.1% (1473)	77.6% (4057)	+ 4.3%
Not Known or Not Applicable	22.3 (72)	16.1 (85)	15.9 (150)	15.4 (231)	15.5 (277)	15.7 (819)	− 7.8
Female	4.6 (15)	5.5 (29)	6.1 (58)	4.2 (63)	7.7 (147)	6.0 (314)	+ 3.1
Male/Female	.3 (1)	—	1.0 (9)	.8 (12)	.7 (14)	.7 (36)	+ .4
Total	100% 323	100% 527	100% 944	100% 1501	100% 1911	100% 5226	

product of husband and wife teams from North America. There do not appear to be very many similar teams in India although recently more men and women are working together in research endeavours. It might be interesting to study these male/female research teams, both foreign and Indian, to discover if functions within the team are dependent to some extent on sex; for example, do women do more of the clerical work necessitated by research although they are in title and salary equal to male co-workers and how men react to the situation where a woman researcher is supposed to be their equal. Will women unconsciously assume a subordinate role on such research teams and are there differences cross-culturally between Indian teams and foreign teams ? It is highly probable, however, that if the trend for greater number of women in research continues, more research teams will have female members.

Although the number of women in sociological research is quite small they are concentrated in particular subject areas. The relationship between sex of author and subject classification was determined by using the chi-square test. The X^2 value was found to be 120.66931 with 23 degrees of freedom and therefore the hypothesized relationship was significant at the .005 level.

It is evident from Table 25 that men and women engaged in Indian Sociological research have been segregated into traditional male and female areas of study. Women have pursued the more family-child oriented types of research, the more genteel subjects such as the sociology of art, language and literature and research of the traditional female professions such as teaching and nursing. The number of women in social psychology does not really represent a departure from traditional research activities of women for although new skills have been learned, women researchers still usually have studied the social psychology of other women, children, adolescents and in a few cases university students. The percentage of women in the Sociology of Science cannot be taken as a field where women are particularly concentrated because there are only two studies by women in this category but because of the small total number the per cent appears high.

It has been shown earlier that men have almost completely dominated Indian sociological research. The subject areas shown on Table 25 however, are those where men have been especially prominent. Men have dominated fields of research that primarily

TABLE 25

Subject Categories where per cent of Research by Male Authors ≤ 90%		
Subject Category	Male	Female
Family and Socialization	82.5%	17.5%
Sociology of the Arts	83.9	16.1
Sociology of Health and Medicine	84.1	15.9
Sociology of Education	87.8	12.2
Social Psychology	81.1	11.9
Sociology of Science	88.2	11.8

Subject Categories where per cent of Research by Male Authors ≥ 95%		
Subject Category	Male	Female
Sociology of Knowledge	100%	0
Planning, Forecasting and Speculation	100	0
Sociology : History and Present State	99.3	.7
Mass Phenomena	97.5	2.5
Group Interactions	97.4	2.6
Rural Sociology	96.5	3.5
Community Development	95.9	4.1
Social Change and Economic Development	95.5	4.5

focus on rural phenomena and are more concerned with business and economics. Men have almost exclusively published works on the course of development in Indian sociology and opinions on which changes they would like to see implemented. Women have not entered into these debates and discussions and have left the direction of Indian sociology to be decided by male colleagues.

SIX

Emerging Patterns in Type of Publication

Since 1947 the most common form of publication for Indian research has been journal articles. There appears to be a peak in number of research findings published in journals during 1953-57. Following this peak, the relative frequency for journal articles has declined to approximately the same level it was at in the first time period. This peak might be partially due to the fact that there was no *Sociological Abstracts'* coverage for 1947-52 therefore it appears that several journal articles are probably not included. The higher relative frequency after 1952 is however, not only due to better bibliographic coverage but also a result of the fact that after and during approximately 1952 many Indian sociological journals began publication as well as other relevant journals published in foreign countries. In the final time period journal articles have declined in absolute number and in relative frequency. One of the causes of this decline may be attributed to the growing importance of other types of publications as well as increase in the number of doctoral dissertations, some of which may be eventually published.

Books have been the form of 15.8% of sociological research publications in India during the past twenty-five years. The peak of 31.9% in the earliest time period is again partially due to the bias introduced by inadequate coverage of journal articles but could also indicate that as the number of journals was small, research findings had few alternatives for publication. In the last ten years the book form of publication has been gaining in relative and absolute frequencies. Perhaps as research facilities expand and Indian sociology accumulates a backlog of experience and attains a degree of sophistication more intensive, detailed and long-term studies would be undertaken of various aspects of Indian society.

Dissertations have increased greatly in absolute number and to a lesser extent in relative number since 1947-52. From Table 26 it appears that in the 1968-72 period the number of dissertations have decreased from previous levels. In truth, this has not happened. The misleading figures have been produced because dissertations for 1971 and 1972 from Indian universities were not available and therefore could not be included. In 1969 there were 270 studies or 14% of total research still under progress in the form of doctoral dissertations, thus it is highly probable that the number of dissertations being completed each year is increasing relative to other types of publications. Research in the form of dissertations then has become increasingly important to Indian sociology.

Book chapters have fluctuated widely in relative frequency but in absolute numbers are generally increasing. The fluctuations may have occurred randomly through the edited books which were available from which to pick out individual chapters. Although it is difficult to determine whether or not this publication form is increasing or decreasing in numbers, it is still possible to conclude that book chapters are of some importance in the publication of Indian sociological research as they have contained 8.1% of the total research output.

The variable which has been called "other" contains publication forms such as short research reports from universities and other institutions and papers presented at conferences and seminars. This category has increased indicating that more research findings on society in India are being reported at national and international sociological conferences and congresses and that Indians have begun to play a more prominent role in these meetings of sociologists. The increase in research reports confirms previous statements that government-funded research centers, especially in India, have contributed to the growth of Indian sociological research as well as research projects undertaken by universities with financial help from the government.

Government reports have declined in importance to sociological research in India. During the first time period the government was most actively involved in research in the form of data collection on social phenomena such as groups of people in India, within particular regions of India and in fields which are government functions such as education. This role of government has not decreased in absolute number but it appears that research is no

TABLE 26

Indian Sociological Research, 1947-1972: Cell Frequencies in per cent and Number and Rank Order (1947-1972) by Type of Publication

Type of Publication	1947-52	1953-57	1958-62	1963-67	1968-72	1947-72	% Change 1947-52 to 1968-72
Journal Article	37.5% (121)	65.1% (343)	55.6% (525)	57.6% (864)	36.7% (701)	48.9% (2555)	— .8%
Book	31.9 (103)	13.7 (72)	11.7 (110)	11.8 (177)	18.4 (351)	15.8 (824)	— 13.5
Dissertation	11.1 (36)	10.6 (56)	17.8 (168)	18.7 (280)	14.3 (273)	15.6 (814)	+ 3.2
Book Chapter	12.7 (41)	5.1 (27)	9.7 (92)	4.9 (73)	9.8 (188)	8.1 (423)	— 2.9
Dissertation in Progress	—	—	—	—	14.1 (270)	5.2 (270)	+ 14.1

							+
Other	3.4 (11)	3·0 (16)	3.6 (34)	5.1 (76)	5.7 (109)	4.7 (246)	+ 2.3
Government Report	2.5 (8)	2.1 (11)	1.1 (10)	1.1 (16)	.5 (9)	1.0 (54)	— 2.0
Not Known	.9 (3)	.4 (2)	.5 (5)	1.0 (15)	.5 (10)	.8 (40)	— .4
Total	100% (323)	100% (527)	100% (944)	100% (1501)	100% (1911)	100% (5226)	

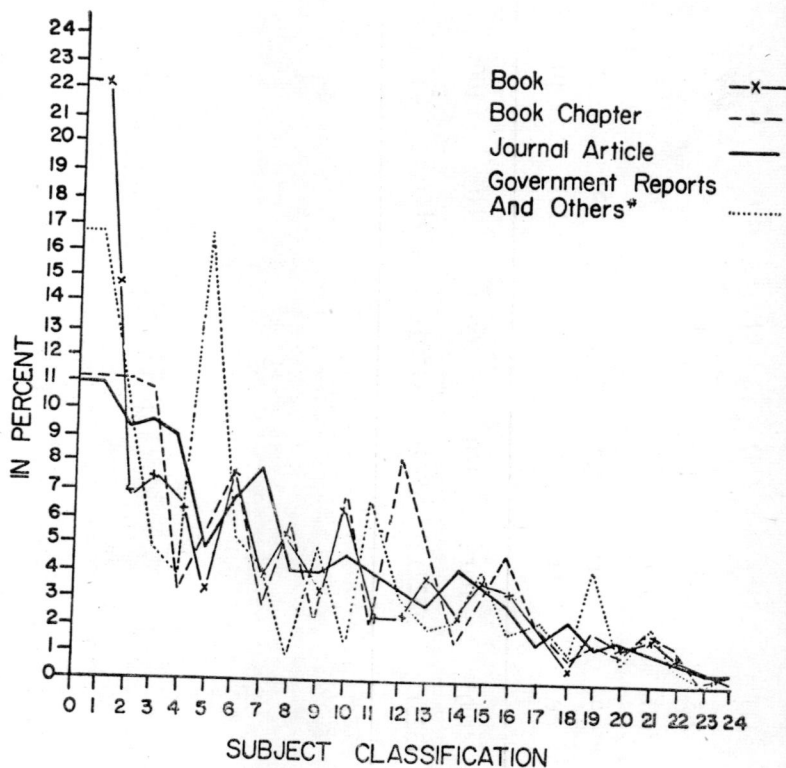

GRAPH IV

Indian Sociological Research; 1947-1972: Frequency
Distribution of Research By Type of Publication.

* classification of others: papers presented at conferences etc.,
research reports.

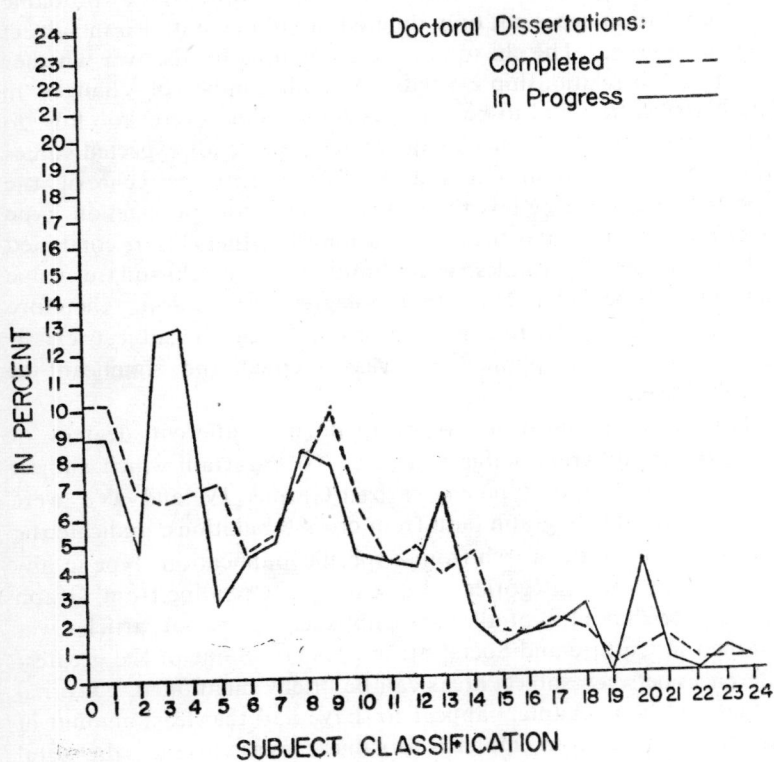

GRAPH IVa

Indian Sociological Research 1947 - 1972 Frequency
Distribution of Research By Type of Publication.

longer a direct responsibility of particular government departments and ministries but that it has been assigned along with financial backing to research centers and universities.

The frequency counts for publication types in each time period provide a picture of how publication types have differed in volume or quantity of research. It was also thought to be quite probable that publication types not only differed in volume but also in subject area emphasis. The chi-square test was used to discover whether or not such a relationship existed. A small number of changes in data classification had to be made as some values were too low to fit the requirements of the chi-square test, where all expected values must be greater than one and at most twenty per cent of the expected values can be less than five. Thus for publication type government reports and the classification of "others" were combined and "not known" variables were omitted. The chi-square value was found to be 581.18213 with 115 degrees of freedom, therefore the hypothesis that there is a relationship between subject classification and type of publication was accepted and significant at the .005 level.

Particular publication types then, give different degrees of emphasis to different subject areas. To ascertain which subject areas each publication type emphasized Graphs IV and IVa were constructed. These graph data from cross-tabulations indicate the percentage of total research from a specific publication type in any of the twenty-four categories. For example a reading from Graph IV might be that 11% of all work published as journal articles was classified in Culture and Social Structure (1). Some of the greatest differences between subject areas can be briefly mentioned. Journal articles and book chapters appear to have had the least amount of variance or have given emphasis to subject areas close to the total amount of emphasis of research in each category. Almost one quarter of all books have been written in Culture and Social Structure. Books have also emphasized Social Differentiation, Social Change and Economic Development and Political Interactions. Government reports have emphasized Culture and Social Structure, Mass Phenomena, Sociology of Education and Methodology and Research Technology. The first three of these subject areas are practical concerns of government for collecting data about the socio-economic conditions of particular groups and tribes in India and for determining how programmes are working and where improvements are needed.   The apparent emphasis on Methodology and Research Technology has been due to the inclusion of seminar proceedings and research reports by government departments. Most of the entries indicated in the cross-classification were papers presented at seminars in India.

Doctoral dissertations, which are from both India and the United States, have emphasized Culture and Social Structure, Mass Phenomena, Complex Organizations and Social Problems and Social Welfare. University students appear to have directed their efforts towards some of the practical problems of moderniza- tion such as the communication and adoption of innovations, industrial development and social problems. Doctoral dissertations in progress in 1969, which are from India, indicate that significant shifts have taken place in the most heavily researched areas. Culture and Social Structure has fallen below the level of pre-viously completed dissertations. Rural Sociology, Mass Phenomena, Political Interactions and Community Development have likewise declined. New areas of emphasis are Social Differentiation, the Family and Socialization, Urban Structures and Ecology and Social Control. These findings generally indicate a trend towards more interest in urban India as opposed to rural and tribal settings and perhaps a greater concern for elements of stability and order in society such as the family, the caste system and laws when these traditional organizational frameworks for Indian society are rapidly changing in form and process.

TRENDS IN JOURNALS

As journals have been shown to be the most dominant channel for researchers to publish their findings, ten Indian journals have been selected for further analysis. The journals chosen are the major Indian sociological journals and have been listed in Table 27 with accompanying figures for relative frequencies and absolute frequencies. Before discussing specific journals some general trends can be mentioned.

All journals have increased in absolute number of articles and all but two have increased relative to the total research output. These figures confirm the fact that publication in journals has significantly increased in importance to Indian sociology, although their importance is now levelling off. Comparisons of Table 27 and Table 26 reveals that out of the 37.5% of total research

TABLE 27

Indian Sociological Research: 1947-1972 : Cell Frequencies of Selected Indian Journals in per cent of Total Research, per cent of Total Number from the Journals and Absolute Number: Arranged in Rank Order from Highest Absolute Number (1947-1972) to Lowest

Name of Journal	1947-52	1953-57	1958-62	1963-67	1968-72	1947-72	%Change 1947-52 to 1968-72
Indian Journal of Social Work	.3%	8.2%	8.3%	5.5%	4.8%	5.7%	+ 4.5%
	4.76%	33.33%	33.8%	26.52%	30.67%	29.8%	+ 25.91%
	1	43	78	83	92	297	+ 91
Man In India	1.9	3.0	2.6	5.7	3.0	3.6	+ 2.1
	28.57	12.4	10.8	27.2	19.33	19.1	— 9.24
	6	16	25	85	58	190	+ 52
Sociological Bulletin	.6	4.9	4.3	2.1	1.4	2.6	+ .8
	9.52	20.16	21.65	10.22	8.67	13.8	— .85
	2	26	50	32	26	137	+ 24
Eastern Anthropologist	2.8	5.7	3.0	2.1	1.5	2.4	— 1.3
	42.29	23.26	12.1	9.9	9.67	12.7	— 32.62
	9	30	28	31	29	127	+ 20

							+
Indian Journal of Social Research	0	0	.6 / 2.6 / 6	1.9 / 9.3 / 29	1.8 / 11.67 / 35	1.3 / 7.0 / 70	+ 1.8 / 11.67 / 35
Indian Sociological Bulletin	0	0	1.3 / 5.19 / 12	1.1 / 5.11 / 16	1.2 / 7.67 / 23	1.0 / 5.1 / 51	+ 1.2 / 7.67 / 23
Journal of Social Research	0	0	.7 / 3.03 / 7	1.5 / 7.4 / 23	1.0 / 6.33 / 19	.9 / 4.9 / 49	+ 1.0 / 6.33 / 19
Economic and Political Weekly (Economic Weekly)	.9 / 14.29 / 3	2.1 / 8.53 / 11	1.3 / 5.19 / 12	.3 / 1.6 / 5	.4 / 2.67 / 8	.7 / 3.9 / 39	− .5 / 11.62 / 5
Contributions to Indian Sociology	0	.6 / 2.33 / 3	1.4 / 5.63 / 13	.5 / 2.6 / 8	.1 / .67 / 2	.5 / 2.6 / 26	+ .1 / .67 / 2
Indian Journal of Sociology	0	0	0	0	.4 / 2.67 / 8	.2 / .9 / 9	+ .4 / 2.67 / 8
Total	6.5% / 100% / 21	24.48% / 100% / 129	24.47% / 100% / 231	20.53% / 100% / 312	15.7% / 100% / 300	19.1% / 100% / 995	

published in journals in 1947-52 only 6.5% of it was included in the selected major Indian journals. In 1968-72 out of the 36.7% of total research published in journals, 15.7% of it was published in the ten journals. There is an indication therefore that although the relative amount of research being published in journals has declined slightly, more of this research is being published in Indian journals that have specialized in publishing sociological research. The remaining 31.5% and 21.0% of research for 1947-52 and 1968-72 respectively was published in foreign journals and other Indian journals that are not specifically sociological in nature.

The journal which has come to be of greatest importance in terms of articles published is the *Indian Journal of Social Work* which has experienced the greatest increases in all three frequencies. This journal appears to be very concerned with current social problems and social change in India but also includes a small number of articles on foreign countries and the application of findings in other countries to the Indian situation. *Man In India*, an anthropological journal that has been in existence since 1921, has increased in relation to total research output and in absolute frequency but has declined in importance relative to the other selected journals. The decline is a result of the growing importance of other journals rather than an absolute decline in the role played by *Man in India* in publication of research findings.

The data given for the *Sociological Bulletin*, the journal of the Indian Sociological Society, must be clarified as the journal did not begin publication until 1952. A more realistic picture might have been presented if the figures for the first time-period were added into the next five years of 1953 to 1957. With this alteration the *Sociological Bulletin* does not increase in absolute number and declines relatively as other new journals begin publication. The *Eastern Anthropologist* has lost much of its importance as a publication outlet for sociological research. Although the number of articles has grown, the increase has been hardly large enough to off-set the commencement of many new journals. This journal is published by the Ethnographic and Folk Culture Society in India and is anthropological in scope.

The *Economic and Political Weekly*, formerly the *Economic Weekly*, is another journal that has declined in relative importance to Indian sociology. The Weekly, like the previously mentioned journals, has maintained its position in absolute number but is not a major outlet as it was earlier containing 14.29% of research published in the ten journals from 1947 to 1952.

The Indian Journal of Social Work, Man In India, The Sociological Bulletin, The Eastern Anthropologist and The Economic and Political Weekly have been published for at least the past twenty years and except for the Economic and Political Weekly all have been the major sociological journals in India. Man In India and the Eastern Anthropologist have declined severly in relative importance. Their decline corresponds to the decline found in the analysis of subject areas where the sub-categories of culture and social anthropology declined by 11% (see Table II). The increase in the Indian Journal of Social Work corresponds to increases in subject areas such as Social Stratification, Social Problems and Social Welfare and the Family and Socialization.

The new journals which have begun publication since approximately 1957 have proposed to fulfil functions in Indian sociology which their editorial boards believe are lacking. The Indian Journal of Social Research has hoped to promote international, inter disciplinary research in sociology, a desire which is similar to that of the Indian Sociological Bulletin (now renamed as International Journal of Contemporary Sociology) which hopes to be an international journal of sociology and social sciences published in Indo-American collaboration. Contributions to Indian Sociology first (1957) attempted to present one particular approach in Indian sociology, that of the editors, but later (Since 1968 new series) proposed to provide a forum for the presentation and discussion of different points of view. The Indian Journal of Sociology, which began publication in 1970, has felt its main purpose would be to promote rigid scholarship. The editorial board of this journal has expressed the opinion in a letter introducing its journal that the journal was badly needed because of the low quality of Indian sociological journals. The journal has stressed that it will try to maintain and develop as wide a scope as possible for a scientific sociology in India, accepting manuscripts on many diverse subjects as long as the research is of a high standard.

The proposed functions of these journals, which have begun publication approximately in the past fifteen years, are indicative of changes in the thought of sociologists in India. Generally, there is the belief that foreign collaboration and inter-disciplinary research are to be desired and promoted that it is no detraction or short-coming if sociology is not narrowly bounded in approach and subject matter. Indian sociologists then, if the policies of new journals are any indication, have chosen to develop a broadminded attitude towards their discipline in regard to the previously mentioned aspects.

In addition to these trends in Indian sociological thinking there has also been concern over the quality of work and level of scholarship. The broad-mindedness of Indian sociologists is also accompanied by, especially in the past five years, a good deal of self-criticism in order   that sociological research be improved and brought up to par with sociology   in foregin countries. The analysis of journals cannot measure whether or not these are only trends in thought and aspirations or if they have been put into widespread practice but nevertheless the presence of these ideas is significant especially considering future trends as thought usually proceeds and foreshadows action in the future.

KEY TO SUBJECT CLASSIFICATION IN GRAPH V
 *1.   Methodology and Research Technology
        Sociology : History and Theory
 *2.   Social Psychology
        Group Interactions
  3.   Culture and Social Structure
  4.   Complex Organization
  5.   Social Change and Economic Development
  6.   Mass Phenomena
  7.   Political Interactions
  8.   Social Differentiation
  9.   Rural Sociology
 10.   Urban Sociology
*11.   Sociology of the Arts, Religion and Education and
        Social Control
 12.   Demography and Human Biology
 13.   The Family and Socialization
 14.   Social Problems and Social Welfare
 15.   Community Development
Categories excluded because their low frequency invalidated chi-square calculations:

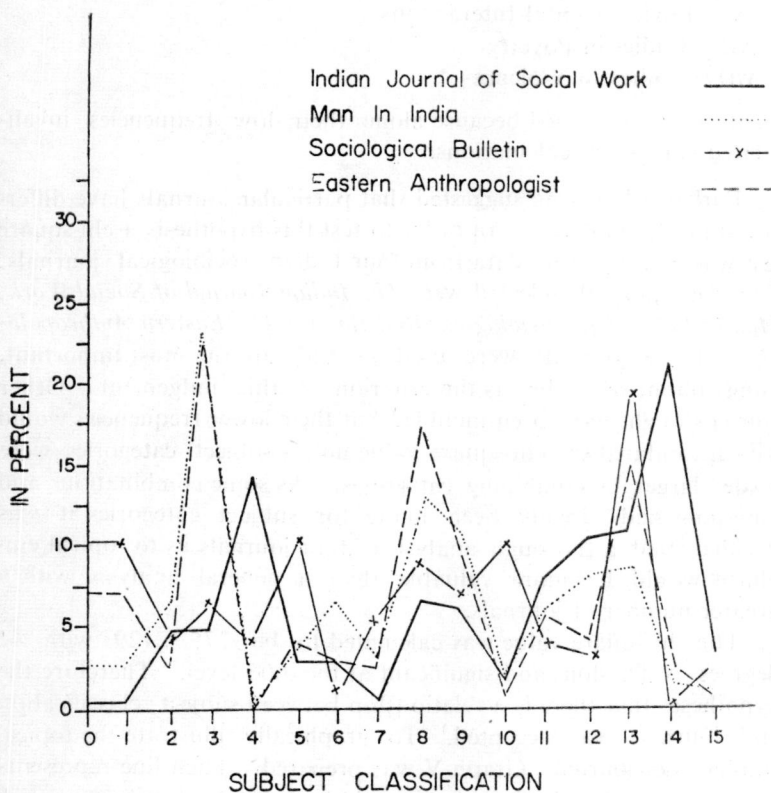

Indian Journal of Social Work ———
Man In India ....
Sociological Bulletin — x —
Eastern Anthropologist — — —

IN PERCENT

SUBJECT CLASSIFICATION

GRAPH V

Indian Sociological Research: 1947 - 1972: Frequency
Distributions of Journals By Subject Classification.

  i)   Sociology of Science
 ii)   Sociology of Health and Medicine
iii)   Sociology of Knowledge
 iv)   Planning, Forecasting and Speculation
  v)   Environmental Interactions
 vi)   Studies in Poverty
vii)   Studies in Violence

*Categories combined because alone their low frequencies invalidated chi-square calculations.

Earlier it has been suggested that particular journals have different topical emphases.   In order to test this hypothesis a chi-square test was performed on data from four Indian sociological journals. The four journals selected were *The Indian Journal of Social Work*, *Man in India*, *The Sociological Bulletin* and *The Eastern Anthropologist*.   These journals were used as they are the most important, using volume of studies as the criterion of this judgement.   Other journals might have been included but their lower frequencies would have invalidated the chi-square value unless subject categories were made larger by combining categories.   As some combinations and omissions had already been made for subject categories it was decided that a thorough analysis of four journals as to topical emphasis would be more valuable than a general analysis with a greater number of journals.

The chi-square value was calculated to be   275.32129   with   42 degrees of freedom and significant at the .005 level.   Therefore the hypotheses that there is a relationship between subject classification and journals was accepted.   To graphically illustrate the topical emphases of journals, Graph V was prepared.   Each line represents the frequency distribution of a journal by subject classification.   A sample reading from the Table might be that out of all the research published in *The Sociological Bulletin*, 19.5% of it was classed as belonging to the Family and Socialization.

The Indian Journal of Social Work was found to have put the most emphasis, compared to the other three journals, on Complex Organizations and Social Problems and Social Welfare and relatively less emphasis on Methodology and Research Technology, Sociology: History and Theory, Social Differentiation, Rural Sociology and Culture and Social Structure.   The journal's emphasis on Social Problems and Social Welfare might be expected considering the nature and objectives of the Journal as expressed in its title. The great number of studies classed in Complex Organizations, upon closer examination, generally dealt with the topics of labour welfare, social security for particular groups of industrial workers, trade unions and employee morale and motivation.

The *Sociological Bulletin* gave major emphasis to the classifications of Methodology and Research Technology and Sociology: History and Present State, Social Change and Economic Development, the Family and Socialization and Urban Structures and Ecology. *The Sociological Bulletin* appears to be fulfilling a vital role in Indian sociology, by publishing several articles on methodology. A breakdown of the cross-tabulations for the first combined category reveals that almost all of these articles have been classed in Sociology: History and Theory, not Methodology and Research Technology. Therefore the *Sociological Bulletin* gives no particular emphasis to methodology but in fact, to the history and present state of sociology. The emphasis on Urban Structures and Ecology could be possibly attributed to the influence of a past editor, G.S. Ghurye, who has shown much interest in urban studies. The greater number of urban studies in the *Sociological Bulletin* is important considering the fact that some scholars believe Indian sociological research to be too rural community oriented. The frequency distribution for *Man In India* and *The Eastern Anthropologist* reflect the stated approach of the journals which is anthropological. A great emphasis has been placed by both journals on Culture and Social Structure. Both journals have also published a great number of studies on Social Differentiation but have contained hardly any work on Complex Organizations and Urban Structures and Ecology. *Man In India* is shown as having the highest proportion of all journals for studies in Mass Phenomena. Most of the articles classified and Mass Phenomena from *Man In India* were in the sub-category of communications and dealt with the diffusion and adoption of innovations especially by tribal people. The majority of these articles were published after 1967.

In general then it can be concluded that most of the important areas of sociological research in India have been given coverage by at least one journal. Some important areas are present however, that have been given little coverage in Indian sociological journals. Such subject areas are Social Psychology and Group Interactions, Mass Phenomena, Political Interactions and Community Development.

With the exception of the *Indian Journal of Social Work*, Complex Organizations and Social Problems and Social Welfare, have received little attention and with the exception of the *Sociological Bulletin*, Social Change and Economic Development and Urban Structures and Ecology have been almost virtually excluded from other journals. Some of these areas conceivably have been given more coverage in other journals, for example Social Change and Economic Development in the *Economic and Political Weekly*.

Mention should also be made of journals which have not been included in this analysis but are significant in that they are edited by sociologists from India. The *International Journal of Comparative Sociology* began publication in India. This journal was edited by K. Ishwaran and it was sponsored by Karnatak University. The journal along with the editor later moved to Canada (York University, Toronto). He also edits the *Journal of Asian and African studies* and *Contributions to Asian Studies*. The *International Journal of Sociology of the Family* and the *International Review of Modern Sociology* are edited by Man Singh Das who is with the Department of Sociology at Northern Illinois University. These two journals are printed in India. Another sociologist from India George Kurian, edits the *Journal of Comparative Family Studies*, from the University of Calgary. These journals are international in scope and have published significant sociological researches.

SEVEN

Significant Directions in Regional Studies

Out of the 5226 entries approximately one-third of them could be classified according to regional variables. Entries that did not have an areal basis, for example, those on methodology, and entries that did not clearly indicate that a particular region was being studied were necessarily excluded. These entries constituted about 29% of the total amount of research. In some cases the titles implied that phenomena throughout all of India were the subjects of study with no special reference to particular regions. Therefore these studies were classified together and comprised approximately 39% of the research.

The remaining 32% of the research was classified according to the different provinces of India listed in Table 28. To make the task of analysis less complicated, to allow for certain computations that were invalidated by low frequencies and to permit wider generalization, regions that are located in proximity to one another were in some cases combined. These groups were then ranked in order from highest to lowest absolute frequency for 1947-1972 and together with absolute and relative frequencies make up Table 28.

Table 28 is quite self-explanatory in indicating which areas are highly, moderately and poorly researched and how the areas of research emphasis have changed in the past twenty-five years. In general, research in almost every region has increased in number as might be expected with the great increased productivity in Indian sociological research discussed earlier (see Table 2 p. 23). Relative frequency changes indicate that broadly speaking northern regions have replaced South India as the major focus of interest and appear to be growing rapidly in importance. Central and Eastern India have been the most poorly researched areas in India but they are not declining in importance as quickly as South India.

Table 28

Indian Sociological Research; 1947-1972 : Cell Frequencies of Regional Groupings in per cent of Total Research, per cent of Total Number from the Regions and Absolute Number : Arranged in Rank Order from Highest Absolute Number (1947-72) to Lowest

Regions	1947-52	1953-57	1958-62	1963-67	1968-72	1947-72	% Change 1947-52 to 1968-72
I Uttar	1.9	2.1	4.4	4.1	6.2	4.6%	+ 4 3
Pradesh	5.3	6.1	13.9	14.2	18.9	14.4	+ 13.6
	6	11	42	62	118	239	+ 112
Bihar	.9	.9	1.5	2.9	2.4	2.1	+ 1.5
	2.6	2.8	4.6	10.1	7.4	6.7	+ 4.8
	3	5	14	44	46	112	+ 43
Delhi	0	.6	.7	.5	.9	.7	+ .9
		1.7	2.3	1.6	2.9	2.1	+ 2.9
		3	7	7	18	35	+ 18
Total	2.8	3.6	6.6	7.5	9.5	7.4	+ 6.7
	7.9	10.6	20.7	25.7	29.1	23.2	+ 21.2
	9	19	63	113	182	386	+ 173

II North India	2.8	4.4	5.3	2.3	3.2	3.4	+ .4
	7.9	12.8	20 7	7.8	9.9	10.7	+ 2.0
	9	23	50	34	62	178	+ 53
Punjab	.6	.9	.6	1.8	1.2	1.2	+ .6
	1.8	2.8	2.0	6.2	3.5	3.7	+ 1.7
	2	5	6	27	22	62	+ 20
Himachal Pradesh	0	.2	0	.3	.4	.3	+ .4
		.6		1.1	1.3	.8	+ 1.3
		1		5	8	14	+ 8
Jammu and Kashmir	0	.6	.1	.2	.1	.2	+ .1
		1.7	.3	.7	.3	.5	+ .3
		3	1	3	2	9	+ 2
Haryana	0	0	0	0	.2	.1	+ .2
					.5	.2	+ .5
					3	3	+ 3
Total	3.4	6.1	6.0	4.6	5.1	5.2	+ 1.7
	9.7	17.8	18.8	15.8	15.5	16 0	+ 5.8
	11	32	57	69	97	266	+ 86

1	2	3	4	5	6	7	8	
III Kerala	3.7	2.1	1.2	.8	1.0	1.3	2.7	—
	10.5	6.1	3.6	2.8	3.2	4.0	7.3	—
	12	11	11	12	20	66	8	+
Karnataka	2.5	2.1	1.2	.4	1.4	1.2	1.1	—
	7.0	6.1	3.6	1.4	4.2	3.7	2.8	—
	8	11	11	6	26	62	18	+
South India	.9	3.4	1.2	.7	.8	1.1	.1	—
	2.6	10.0	3.6	2.5	2.4	3.5	.2	—
	3	18	11	11	15	58	12	+
Tamil Nadu	1.2	1.7	.6	.3	.8	.8	.4	—
	3.5	5.0	2.0	1.1	2.6	2.4	.9	—·
	4	9	6	5	16	40	12	+
Total	2.3	8.3	4.2	2.2	4.0	4.4	4.3	—
	23.7	27.2	12.8	7.8	12.3	13.6	10.4	—
	27	49	39	34	77	226	50	+

IV West Bengal	3.4	2.8	2.4	2.4	2.8	2.7	—	.6
	9.7	8.3	7.6	8.2	8.6	8.4	—	1.1
	11	15	23	36	54	139	+	43
Assam	.6	1.1	.6	1.2	1.0	1.0	+	.4
	1.8	3.3	2.0	4.1	3.0	3.1	+	1.2
	2	6	6	18	19	51	+	17
Nagaland	.3	.4	.1	.1	.2	.2		.1
	.9	1.1	.3	.2	.6	.5		.3
	1	2	1	1	4	9	+	3
Manipur	0	0	0	.1	.3	.1	+	.3
				.2	.8	.4	+	.8
				1	5	6	+	5
NEFA	0	.2	.3	.1	.1	.1	+	.1
		.6	1.0	.2	.2	.4	+	.2
		1	3	1	1	6		1
Sikkim	0	0	.1	.1	0	.1		0
			.3	.5		.2		
			1	2		3		
Tripura	0	0	.1	0	0	0		0
			.3			.1		
			1			1		

1	2	3	4	5	6	7	8
Total	4.3	4.5	3.6	4.0	4.4	4.2	+ .1
	12.3	13.3	11.5	13.5	13.3	12.9	+ 1.0
	14	24	35	59	83	215	+ 69
V Rajasthan	1.5	.8	.7	2.5	1.5	1.6	+ 0
	4.4	3.8	2.3	8.7	4.5	5.0	+ .1
	5	4	7	38	29	83	+ 24
Gujarat	1.5	.9	1.9	1.2	.9	1.2	— .6
	4.4	2.8	5.9	4.1	2.9	3.9	— 1.5
	5	5	18	18	18	64	+ 13
Western India	0	.8	.2	.1	.4	.3	+ .4
		2.2	.7	.5	1.3	1.0	+ 1.3
		4	2	2	8	16	+ 4
Total	3.0	2.5	2.8	3.8	2.8	3.1	— .2
	8.8	7.2	8.9	13.3	8.8	9.8	0
	10	13	27	58	55	163	+ 45

VI Madhya Pradesh	1.9	1.3	1.8	2.0	2.0	1.9	+ .1
	5.3	3.9	5.6	6.9	6.2	6.0	+ .9
	6	7	17	30	39	99	+ 33
Central India	2.5	.6	1.0	1.0	.4	.8	− 2.1
	7.0	1.7	3.0	3.4	1.1	2.5	− 5.9
	8	3	.9	14	7	42	− 1
Total	4.4	1.9	2.8	3.0	2.4	2.7	− 2.0
	12.3	5.6	8.6	10.3	7.6	8.5	− 4.7
	14	10	26	45	46	141	+ 32
VII Orissa	1.2	1.3	1.2	1.0	1.0	1.1	− .2
	3.5	3.9	3.6	3.4	3.0	3.4	− .5
	4	7	11	15	19	56	+ 15
Andhra Pradesh	2.2	.6	.5	1.0	1.3	1.1	− .9
	6.1	1.7	1.6	3.4	4.0	3.3	− 2.1
	7	3	5	15	25	55	+ 18
Eastern India	0	0	.2	.1	0	.1	0
			.7	.2		.2	
			2	1		3	

1	2	3	4	5	6	7	8
Total	3.4	1.9	1.9	2.1	2.3	2.3	— 1.1
	9.7	5.6	5.9		7.0		— 2.7
	11	10	18	31	44	114	+ 33
VIII Maharashtra	5.6	4.4	4.1	1.8	2.0	2.8	— 3.6
	15.8	12.8	12.8	7.1	6.2	6.9	— 9.6
	18	23	39	27	39	146	+ 21
Goa	0	0	0	.1	.2	.1	+ .2
				.2	.5	.2	+ .5
				1	3	4	+ 3
Total	5.6	4.4	4.1	1.9	2.3	2.9	+ 3.3
	15.8	12.8	12.8	6.4	6.7	9.0	— 9.1
	18	23	39	28	42	150	+ 24
TOTAL	35.2%	34.2%	32.2%	29.1%	32.8%	32.2%	— 3.0
	100%	100%	100%	100%	100%	100%	
	114	180	304	437	626	1661	+ 1547

Moderately researched areas have been Western India and North-east India (Region IV in Table 28).

Some reasons might be offered for the variance in relative frequencies for regions. North India and South India (Regions I, II and III) are probably the most heavily researched areas because they are the most densely populated regions in India. They are also quite industrialized and urbanized compared to the rest of India, a fact which may not influence research directly, but is usually a prerequisite for the development and growth of universities. If there are universities in a particular area they will probably, although not always, study the immediate surroundings and conduct research in the state or city in which they are located. An examination of Indian universities in the *Commonwealth Universities Yearbook* for 1972 revealed that there are almost twice as many universities that offer instruction in sociology and related social sciences in the north (Regions I and II) then there are in the south (Region III). Areas that had the fewest universities that offered sociology and related disciplines were in East India (Region VIII) and North-east India (Region V). Maharashtra and Madhya Pradesh had slightly higher numbers of universities but they were usually concentrated in only one or a few cities such as Bombay. There was an equal number of institutions offering sociology and related disciplines in Rajasthan and Gujarat as there were in South India.

The difference between South India and North India in that the number of studies in South India are declining in relative frequency whereas studies on North India are increasing, is surprising considering that in recent years many new sociology departments have been created in southern universities. It is possible that in spite of the growth of sociology in southern universities, sociological research has not increased that rapidly on South India because the universities do not have the accumulated experience that northern universities have in research and that because of strained finances scholars are more confined to fulfilling teaching obligations and the "luxury" of research cannot be afforded. Sociology departments in the south also are smaller in number of teaching staff and most likely student enrolment. In all the proper atmosphere and conditions that attract people interested in research have not yet developed in most southern universities therefore the area has not been greatly studied as researchers go elsewhere.

Table 29

Indian Sociological Research, 1947—1972: Regional Groups by Nationality of Authors

Regional Groups	Indian	North American	United Kingdom	European	Total
I Uttar Pradesh, Delhi, Bihar	348	21	1	0	370
II North India, Jammu & Kashmir, Punjab, Himachal Pradesh, Haryana	178	58	8	6	250
III West Bengal, Assam, Nagaland, Manipur, Tripura, Sikkim, NEFA	192	11	2	1	206
IV Karnataka, Kerala, Tamil Nadu, South India	132	51	8	6	187
V Rajasthan, Gujarat, West India	134	7	4	1	146
VI Maharashtra, Goa	124	18	0	0	142
VII Madhya Pradesh, Central India	105	14	5	6	130
VIII Orissa, Eastern India, Andhra Pradesh	93	6	7	2	108

Regional variations were also present in regions studied by Indians and foreigners in the subject categories researched in particular regions. Table 29 gives a breakdown of authors' nationality by regional groups in absolute frequency. Areas that have attracted most of the foreigners are North India (Region I and II) and secondly, South India (Region III). Other areas have had much smaller numbers of foreign researchers except for, to some extent, Maharashtra and Goa. Foreigners then, have usually tended to stay in areas near to bigger Indian cities such as Bombay, Delhi, Lucknow, Bangalore and Madras. It is probable that in the bigger cities and more urbanized areas better research facilities exist for the use of foreigners as well as the cities being more cosmopolitan in nature which allows foreigners to adjust to their new surroundings more easily. More foreigners have researched in the north than in the south because they are nearer to the most important cities in India such as the capital city of Delhi.

A relationship between subject classification and region was found through the use of the chi-square test. The chi-square value was calculated to be 307.09277 with 98 degrees of freedom and therefore significant at the .005 level. Most regions had their highest frequencies in the subject areas that were the most highly researched (see Graphs VI and VIa). The most significant differences between lines is therefore when a sizable departure is made by a point from the usual clustering of the other points. Studies on Uttar Pradesh, Delhi and Bihar were unique from the general distribution in that they were high in Complex Organizations, Urban Structures and Ecology and Social Problems and Social Welfare and to a lesser extent Demography and Human Biology. Region II of North India, Jammu & Kashmir, Punjab, Himachal Pradesh and Haryana was extremely high in Culture and Social Structure. Karnataka, Kerala, Tamil Nadu and South India, in contrast to the two northern regional groups, had fewer extreme values and were low in the previously mentioned subject classifications for Uttar Pradesh, Delhi and Bihar. Emphasis in South India has been on Culture and Social Structure, Social Differentiation, Sociology of Religion, Education and the Arts and Social Control and the Family and Socialization, although not to a greater extent than other regions. The contrast between North and South Indian research then is not only in number and amount of foreigners but also in subject areas. It is quite surprising that

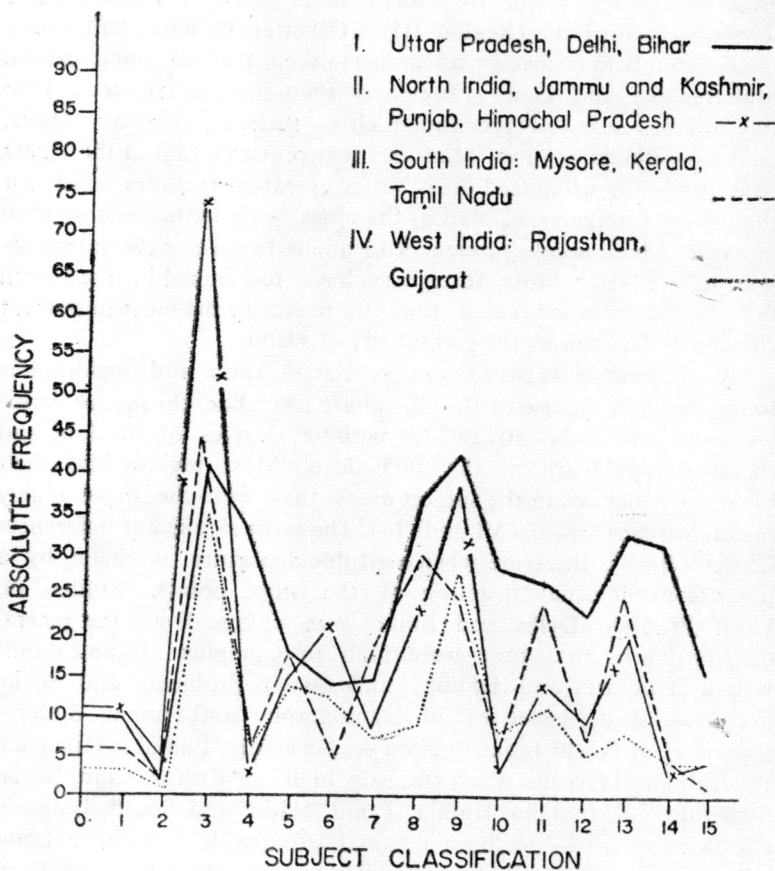

GRAPH VI

Indian Sociological Research; 1947 - 1972: Frequency Distribution For Regional Groups By Subject Classification.

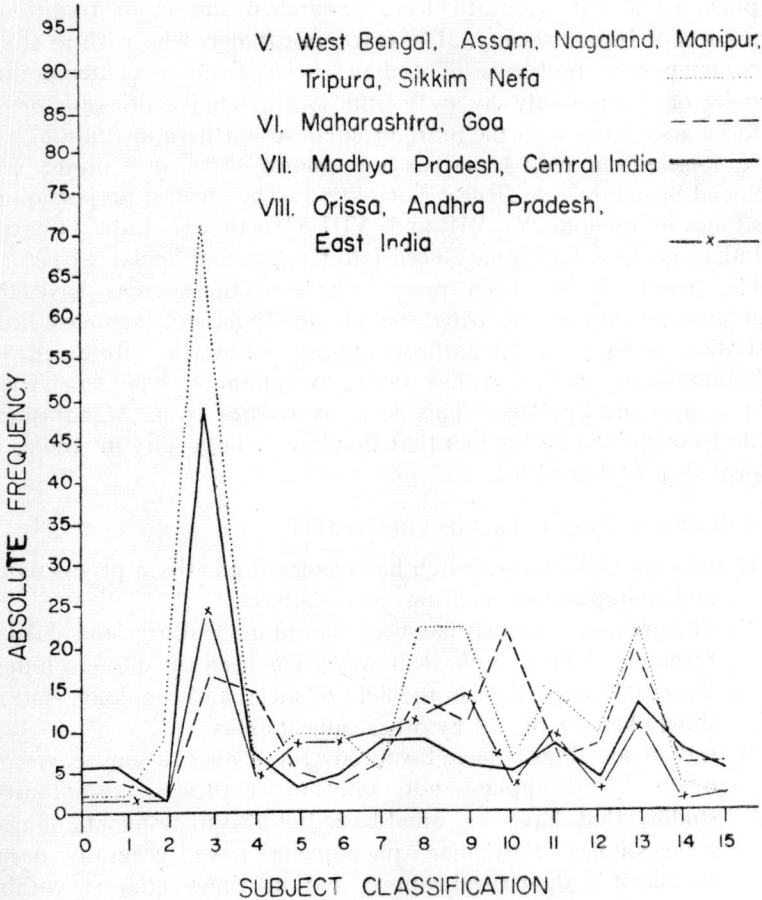

V. West Bengal, Assam, Nagaland, Manipur,
   Tripura, Sikkim Nefa

VI. Maharashtra, Goa

VII. Madhya Pradesh, Central India

VIII. Orissa, Andhra Pradesh,
     East India

GRAPH VIa

Indian Sociological Research: 1947 - 1972: Frequency
Distribution For Regional Groups By Subject Classification

these differences in subject areas exist considering that both regions are almost equally urbanized and industrialized. The researchers in South India have not yet studied these modern phenomena but seem to have researched the more traditional aspects of Indian society. Therefore, researchers who wish to study contemporary problems of Indian society from a contemporary point of view possibly shy away from southern universities and prefer to be associated with the more progressive northern institutions.

Research in West India has been mainly done in Culture and Social Structure and Rural Sociology. The greatest proportion of studies in Regions V, VII and VIII (North-east India, Central India and East India) have been into Culture and Social Structure. This emphasis has been present because these areas have the greatest proportion of tribal people in India and they have been studied using a social anthropological approach. Research in Maharashtra and Goa has been exceptionally high in Urban Structures and Ecology. This peak in studies from Maharashtra can be explained by the fact that Bombay, a large city in India, is located in Maharashtra.

SUMMARY OF MAJOR TRENDS (1947-1972)

(1) Indian sociological research has increased greatly in productivity and in importance as a university subject.

(2) The greatest emphasis has been placed on Culture and Social Structure. This emphasis however has been steadily declining since 1947, especially in the field of social anthropology, and is slowly being replaced by other subject areas.

(3) Indian sociologists have favoured rural over urban environments. This applies not only to small-scale community studies that have an areal basis but also to systematic large-scale studies. Particular phenomena have generally been examined in their rural context and at times ignored within the urban context. In recent years, however, urban studies have grown in number and have been directed towards contemporary urban problems.

(4) Social change in relation to economic development has been studied more thoroughly in recent years. Many important aspects of society though, have still not been intensively examined in regard to their present day dynamics and the problems produced.

(5)   Indian sociological research has often served a practical purpose for government. Throughout the twenty five year period, but especially in the first ten years, sociologists were employed by the government mainly to gather data and confined their analysis to description. In later years, sociologists have worked for the government to the greatest extent through government funded research projects. Their analyses however still do not stress cognitive analysis or explanation. Sociologists generally have not served the practical needs of government by conducting cause and effect type studies that give government a comprehensive basis for decision and policy making.

(7)   Research has come to be more dominated by Indian authors who publish their articles in Indian journals and have their books published by Indian publishing houses. American scholars have retained almost the same proportion of research as they did in 1947-52 but British researchers have declined greatly in number, as has Britain as a place of publication. America has become slightly more important as a place of publication.

(8)   Women researchers are growing slowly in number and with a few exceptions, have played a minor role in sociological research. They have been segregated as to subject areas, that is, following traditional female topics of interest. Their main contribution to sociology has been in these traditional fields as well as teachers of sociology at the university level.

(9)   Journals have become increasingly important. They are filling a vital role in Indian sociological research in that progressive editorial policies have been recently adopted. These policies undoubtedly will directly and indirectly influence research so that research will reflect the policies.
Anthropological journals have decreased greatly in importance as a publication outlet for sociological research.

(10) Northern India has been better researched than southern India especially in fields that deal with forces of modernization such as urbanization and industrialization.

(11) Research teams and foreign collaboration are slowly growing and are being encouraged and promoted. Foreign collaboration however, has not lead to increased cross cultural studies except in a few cases.

KEY TO SUBJECT CLASSIFICATION ON TABLES

1. Social Psychology
2. Group Interactions
3. Culture and Social Structure
4. Complex Organizations
5. Social Change and Economic Development
6. Mass Phenomena
7. Political Interactions
8. Social Differentiation
9. Rural Sociology
10. Urban Structures and Ecology
* 11. Sociology of Religion, Education, and the Arts and Social Control
12. Demography and Human Biology
13. The Family and Socialization
14. Social Problems and Social Welfare
15. Community Development

Categories excluded because they are not regional in scope and because their low frequency invalidated chi-square calculations :

(i) Methodology and Research Technology
(ii) Sociology : History and Theory
(iii) Sociology of Science
(iv) Sociology of Health and Medicine
(v) Sociology of Knowledge
(vi) Planning, Forecasting and Speculation
(vii) Environmental Interactions
(viii) Studies in Poverty
(ix) Studies in Violence

* Categories here combined because alone their low frequencies invalidated chi-square calculations.

EIGHT

Content Analysis of Sociological Journals: Select Subject Areas

INTRODUCTION

The preceding analysis was designed to bring to light general trends for the variables of subject area, nationality of author, place of publication, journals and regions. Only the information provided by bibliographic entries was used. Earlier our quantitative analysis of sociological research productivity in India (1947-1972) by type of publication revealed that the largest portion of research, i.e. 48.9% was published in the form of journal articles (vide, Table 27). It was decided therefore to conduct a more indepth analysis of subject areas selected as being most important because of the volume of studies in each area published in Indian sociological journals. The subject areas chosen are as follows:

I   Culture and Social Structure
    (a)   social organization
    (b)   culture
    (c)   social anthropology (and ethnology)
II   Social Differentiation
    (a)   social stratification
    (b)   sociology of occupations and professions
III   Community Studies
    (a)   rural sociology
    (b)   communications
    (c)   community development
    (d)   urban sociology
IV   The Family and Socialization
    (a)   sociology of the child and socialization
    (b)   adolescence and youth
    (c)   sociology of sexual behaviour

(d)   sociology of the family
(e)   family planning
V   Social Change and Economic Development
(a)   social change and economic development
(b)   market structures and consumer behaviour

For each of the five categories, all entries that had been published in any of the ten Indian sociological journals listed in Table 27 were selected. From these lists of journal articles for each subject area, a random sample of size fifty was drawn using random number tables. Each subject area consisted of articles from sub-categories of varying size in numerical frequency. It was assumed that as each journal article has a probability of being selected proportionate to the size of the sub-categories under which they are classified, the sample of size fifty would accurately represent the real distribution of articles by sub-category in each subject area.

The method of selecting articles from Indian sociological journals was used because the vast majority of abstracts of these articles were found in the *Sociological Abstracts*. This meant that even though the majority of articles were not readily available in complete form, there was a concise summary of them available for analysis. In a few cases where articles had been selected that were published in 1972, the actual journal article was consulted as no *Sociological Abstracts'* coverage was yet available. Unfortunately, as neither *Sociological Abstracts'* coverage nor the actual articles were available for 1947-52 studies published in these five years were omitted from the analysis.

Information from the *Sociological Abstracts* essentially answered the questions of what authors did, how they did it and what conclusions were drawn. The data collected were found to fall into general classification schemes that shall be discussed for each subject area. Information regarding what authors did or phenomena studied, for example, fell into the classification system of subject sub-categories whereas for how authors did their research, new schemes were derived.

CULTURE AND SOCIAL STRUCTURE

The subject area of Culture and Social Structure was analyzed as to how authors conducted research in light of their method of data collection. The classification system used and results are presented in Table 30.

TABLE 30

Method of Data Collection	Number of Articles
A. Empirical Sources	
(i) Primary data	31
(ii) secondary data	5
(iii) both primary and secondary data	5
B. Historical Sources	
(i) sacred	2
(ii) secular	0
C. Speculative Philosophical	1
D. Policy Research	
(i) for government planners, etc.	1
(ii) for sociologists, anthropologists	2
E. Empirical—Speculative	1
F. Empirical—Historical	2
Total	50

It is obvious from Table 30 that Indian sociological research relating to Culture and Social Structure has been overwhelmingly empirical, especially considering the use of primary data. This finding is understandable considering that the majority of articles are social and cultural anthropological in nature and therefore employ the methods of these disciplines which are dominated by field research. Both of the articles classed as using historical source material were investigations into aspects of social structure in Ancient India. Articles classed as policy research for government were those wherein sociologists hoped to clear up misconceptions of pl nners and administrators and give social and cultural anthropology direction as to how problems should be selected for study. The article that was empirical and speculative attempted to explain empirical findings and gave a possible conclusion. The

148   THE SOCIOLOGY OF CONTEMPORARY INDIA

empirical-historical articles were examinations of present day phenomena to which historical data are very relevant for their study such as the institutions of *Panji* or system of preserving geneologies among the Maithil Brahmans.[1] The article classed as speculative-philosophical was an examination of cultural relativism and the relationship of cultures and their values to the needs of society.

The number of empirical studies using primary data was further analyzed considering various techniques used by social scientists. The techniques and results are presented in Table 31.

TABLE 31

Technique	Number of Articles
A. Field Research	32
B. Surveys	
(i) interviews	1
(ii) questionnaires	1
(iii) not specifically stated	2
C. Participant Observation	1
D. Records	0
E. Surveys and Records	1
Total	38

Again the orientation of data collection is very clear, that is, towards the technique of field research. This category is disadvantageous because of its generality but was necessitated by the inadequate amount of data provided by the *Sociological Abstracts*. It may be assumed that field research by social and cultural anthropologists in India frequently has entailed participant observation although it is only in one case that the *Sociological Abstracts* specifically states the use of this technique. In a small number of studies, data were collected through the use of interviews and questionnaires. In one case it appears that informal interviews were conducted with heads of lineage groups in order to investigate the early settlement of a village as no authentic records existed.[2] In another article data were collected about a number of tribal families regarding various social and economic facts, to ascertain social changes and continuity.[3] Two studies classed under social organization made use of surveys, one taking a survey of nuclear households and another using a scale in order to measure social distance. The general survey category was used when it was not clear whether interviews or questionnaires had been used.

The methods used by authors to reach their conclusions have also been analyzed considering the degree of quantification. For this analysis a four class scale was used that rated studies by degree of quantification. The four classes were those devised by P. Chakrabarti[4] in his article "Quantification and Social Research: A Trend Analysis."

They are as follows:

1 Collection of data: without application of any sampling procedure
   presentation of data: without any quantification

2 Collection of data: same as 1
   presentation of data: elementary quantification in the form of frequency distributions, percentages etc.

3 Collection of data: some form of sampling techniques
   presentation of data: same as 2

4 Collection of data: same as 3
   presentation of data : same as 2 plus application of some statistical tests to draw valid inferences.

Each of the fifty articles for this analysis of Culture and Social Structure were classified according to the abovementioned scheme. Table 32 shows the results obtained.

From Table 32 it is obvious that studies in Culture and Social Structure have been primarily qualitative, collecting data with no use of sampling procedures and presenting data without any quantitative analysis. This again seems to be what might be expected considering the traditional approach of social and cultural anthropology and the main objectives of studies in this subject area which often are not conducive to quantitative analysis, for example discussing process of acculturation or tribal rites and customs. The studies that were classified in any group greater than 1 were all in the sub-category of social organization except for two articles from social anthropology which were classed as 2.

TABLE 32

Degree of Quantification	Number of Articles
1	42
2	6
3	1
4	1
Total	50

The articles from social structure classed as 2 did not use sampling procedures but did make use of percentages and frequency counts for presentation of findings such as percentage of people born in kin groups and percentage married into kin groups. The articles classed as 3 and 4 made use of sampling procedures as well as quantitative manipulation of data such as the use of scales and statistically calculated coefficients of correlation.

Out of the fifty sample studies in Culture and Social Structure only six have explicitly made use of existing theories or have contributed to the building of new theories. The word explicitly has been used as much research indirectly uses theoretical constructs in the collection of data and its manipulation but makes no acknowledgement of any specific theory. For example, when seeking to explain a particular phenomena, a researcher chooses variables believed to have some bearing on the phenomena. Implicitly then, there is a theory guiding the researcher in higher selection of variables although it has not yet been stated explicitly or formally. Two studies in the sub-category of social organization were found to base part of their analysis on previously developed theoretical frameworks, for example, regarding cross-cousin marriage.

The four other studies were drawn from culture and social anthropology and were considered to be contributions to theoretical knowledge. The nature of these theoretical contributions can be briefly mentioned. One researcher hoped to offer a theory of a possible route for migration based on findings of cultural similarities between tribal groups in India and Australian aborigines.[5] Another endeavoured to present a theory for the origin and existence of tribal hunters and gatherers not necessarily applicable only to the Indian context.[6] A type of theoretical contribution was made in the formulation of a seven-fold typology of tribes. This typology, however, was suggested only on the basis of two ethnographic studies for tribal Bihar, and therefore was quite limited in applicability.[7] Finally, a theoretical contribution was made by a study on cultural relativism which offered a theoretical concept for the study of cultures and their values.[8] Despite the use of these theoretical concepts and in some cases their formulation, Indian sociological research in the field of Culture and Social Structure has remained largely idiographic.

The form of research where hypotheses are firstly established, tested, and then rejected or accepted has only been utilized in a modified form in two articles out of the fifty. These two studies were also theoretical in nature and endeavoured to clarify particular generalizations with specific reference to India. As an example, reference may be made to the article mentioned earlier, which dealt with the origin and continuing existence of tribal hunters and gatherers and hoped to refute old ideas regarding these areas of research. Studies then, have not been structured in the fashion of setting up hypotheses for analysis or in the method characteristic of most American empirical and quantitative research. Indian sociological research in the subject area of Culture and Social Structure has not followed this type of inquiry and instead has been descriptive discussions of phenomena that are not specifically areas of controversy. The research then essentially has not been problem-oriented in nature and has hoped to relate or describe rather than interpret and explain.

Information was available from the *Sociological Abstracts* about the areal perspective taken by authors. The data has been summarized and tabulated in Table 33.

TABLE 33

Areal Unit of Study	Number of Articles
A. Micro; any area smaller than or equal to an Indian state	40
B. Tribal areas that are contained in more than one state;	
(i) empirical-primary data	0
(ii) other	3
C. All India	
(i) empirical-primary data	0
(ii) other	3
D. Not Applicable	4
Total	50

In forty articles out of the sample size of fifty it was found that observations were made and conclusions drawn for micro units of study such as villages, small areas such as valleys and in some cases states. There were no articles that attempted to gather primary data for larger units of study although a small number made use and described many aspects of their social and economic life and the changes these aspects have recently undergone. Much research was also directed towards examination of tribal ceremonies and rites. A smaller number of researchers have studied rural non-tribal villages using the social anthropological framework and according to this sample, no research of this nature (social anthropological) has been done in urban areas. Recently, some anthropologists in India have suggested areas of research that need more attention. Their emphasis has been on studying tribal customs, ways of life and groups that have not been recorded but are rapidly disappearing in the wake of modernization and on arriving at some theoretical understanding of tribal groups as well as the totality of Indian society and culture.

Studies in social organization have usually approached the study of Indian social systems by basing analysis on familial units such as nuclear households, joint families, kinship groups and clans. Caste organization as a part of total social organization has been discussed. Kinship terminology has been researched as it reflects social organization patterns. Some attention has been focused on social structure in ancient India and the development of particular social roles through time.

Cultural studies have dealt mainly with the problems of tribal integration and acculturation in Hindu society and the Indian nation in general. Some research has been concerned with the question of how cultural studies should be undertaken within a changing society. N.K. Bose has made noteworthy contributions to this area of cultural studies.[9] Tribal transformation as a focus for cultural studies has resulted in the identification of various factors that influence change and the processes of change that are essentially traditional such as Hinduization and Sanskritization and modern forces such as Christianity and urbanization.

Summary of Important Trends: Culture and Social Structure

(1) Research has been dominated by empirical studies which employ primary data that has been collected through fieldwork.

(2) The field research has been rarely conducted with the use of statistical aids nor has data been presented quantitatively.

(3) Research has remained extremely idiographic and theoretical developments have been quite meagre.

(4) Research has been empirical more so in the traditions of British anthropology than in the tradition of American empiricism where hypotheses are established and tested and more quantification has been apparent.

(5) Topical emphasis has been on tribal groups which have been studied on the basis of micro areal units.

SOCIAL DIFFERENTIATION

The subject area of Social Differentiation, containing the subcategories of social stratification and the sociology of occupations and professionals, was analyzed according to methods of data collection. The results are presented in Table 34.

TABLE 34

Method of Data Collection	Number of Authors
A. Empirical Sources	
(i) primary data	21
(ii) secondary data	11
(iii) both primary and secondary data	5
B. Historical Sources	
(i) sacred	1
(ii) secular	2
C. Speculative-Philosophical	1
D. Policy—research	
(i) for government planners, etc.	2
(ii) for sociologists, anthropologists	2
E. Empirical—Speculative	1
F. Empirical—Historical	4
Total	50

Almost half of the total number of sample articles were found to utilize data which were empirical and primary. One-third of these articles had been classified as belonging to the sociology of occupations and professions and dealt mainly with occupational aspirations and mobility as well as one socio-economic survey of an occupational group. The articles which were classed as belonging to social stratification all were concerned with aspects of the caste system. Empirical studies of the caste system using primary data often were descriptions of caste patterns in villages or other settings as well as examinations of changes in caste structure and the relationship between occupation and caste.

Studies which were empirical but used secondary data are also quite substantial in number. Such articles appeared to suggest a degree of unity within the study of social differentiation in India as researchers build on each other's conclusions and relate their findings to the total accumulated body of knowledge. A smaller number of articles have been based on both primary and secondary data.

Often the primary data had been collected through the author's first hand experience with a particular phenomena, for example, one researcher discussed sociologists as a professional, occupational group and based part of his analysis on observation made as a participant in sociological conferences.[10]

Data from historical sources are also significant to the study of social differentiation in India. This is understandable in light of the nature of the caste system as a social order outlined in sacred texts hundreds of years ago. Other historical sources have been used though besides sacred texts such as historical accounts of particular groups in India and recent histories of phenomena such as caste organizations and ideas of Westerners in the past three hundred years on slavery. A combination of historical and empirical data has been the case in some articles where some aspects of social differentiation were studied from the point of view of their history and then in their present day state.

Policy research has been of lesser importance along with research that is speculative and philosophical in nature. Policy research for governmental purposes has attempted to answer questions and give recommendations for problems such as national integration and the management of workers in industries by personnel officers. Policy research for sociologists has been directed towards deriving the proper conceptual framework for the study of caste. Both articles classed as policy research for sociologists were by foreigners or non-Indians. Although this apparent interest by foreigners in problems in studying caste appears to outweigh that of Indians no inferences will be made as the sample of research articles is small and from a restricted source, i.e. only journal articles.

Studies using empirical, primary data were further analyzed to ascertain techniques of data collection, the results of which are presented in Table 35.

Both field research and surveys have been major techniques for data collection. Articles based on field research have generally been examination of caste system that were descriptive analyses where conclusions were arrived at through the author's observations of what has transpired before him. The method used often appears to be participant observation but is not specifically mentioned by the *Sociological Abstracts*. The caste system and various occupational groups have been surveyed in many instances to draw conclusions about them. Surveys have generally yielded quantitative information and have been based on scales and levels such as scales of caste ranking and levels of aspiration.

TABLE 35

Technique	Number of Articles
A. Field Research	14
B. Surveys	
(i) interviews	3
(ii) questionnaires	5
(iii) not specifically stated	3
C. Participant Observation	1
D. Records	1
E. Surveys and Records	0
Total	27

The amount of quantification was determined for Social Differentiation through the use of the quantitative-qualitative continuum referred to earlier.

TABLE 36

Degree of Quantification	Number of Articles
1	38
2	3
3	6
4	3
Total	50

Again, as was found for Culture and Social Structure, the vast majority of articles in Social Differentiation were qualitative or used no sampling procedure and no quantification. Some researchers however have adopted quantitative techniques. Almost all of the articles in the third degree of quantification had been research in the sociology of occupation and professions, not social stratification, which in this analysis is synonymous with the caste system. It is perhaps possible that occupational groups are more conducive to quantification than caste groups as boundaries are clearer. The possibility is also present that the sociology of occupations and professions is more quantitative than social stratification because the fundamentals of the subject area have been imported from the West to a greater extent than the frameworks guiding research into caste.

The three articles utilizing quantitative techniques classed as 4, used sampling procedures such as stratified random samples as well as statistical tests to draw inferences. Statistical tests, generally. employed were the chi-square test and rank-order coefficients of correlation. Articles which were classed as using the second degree of quantification were primarily quantitative in that responses from interviewers and questions were tabulated to yield percentages and in one case sociograms.

Out of the fifty articles, seven were found either to make use of existing theories or to contribute to the building of theories. Two articles were considered contributions to theory building. One hoped to outline a new componential model of caste in contrast to previously stated theories of caste which made use of an ideal type caste system.[11] The other article hoped to present a theoretical approach to the study of minorities in India using Western theoretical development as a basis.[12]

Three articles used the existing theory of an ideal Varna system. Comparisons were made to the ideal type in light of present day workings of the caste system.[13] In another case some mention was made of reference group theory and its use in studying caste and occupational mobility in village India.[14] Another article attempted to study the institution of slavery in society by utilizing a theory of the progress of mankind, that is, from savagery to barbarism to civilization.[15]

On the whole sociological research in India in Social Differentiation has made only moderate progress towards the development of theoretical concepts. Most theoretical concepts found within the sample articles either drew on the traditional, ideal type of caste system or a concept of what caste should be like theoretically according to religious literature or made reference to and based arguments on theories developed in the West, particularly America. It appears that contemporary theories of the caste system which are solely the product of Indian minds have not been forthcoming. Much reliance has been exhibited on American theoretical concepts without an equal reliance on the development of a body of theoretical knowledge by Indian sociologists.

Hypotheses testing has not been a common form for research in the study of Social Differentiation. Three articles were organized around the proving or disproving of hypotheses through the use of statistical tests. Hypotheses therefore were stated in terms that were readily conducive to measurement. An example of such a hypothesis might be the higher the level of education, the higher the occupational aspiration.

Four other articles examined particular hypotheses but conducted the analyses qualitatively. Generally these articles hoped to dispel some aspects of social stratification which the authors felt were erroneous. Phenomena studied in this manner were the self-sufficiency of villages in light of the complementary roles played by nomads, whether or not there are class or caste distinctions of tribals, and precise concepts of the caste system which should be adopted for guidance in research.

Table 37 shows the breakdown of data from the fifty articles by areal perspective taken by authors.

TABLE 37

Areal Unit of Study	Number of Articles
A. Micro; any area smaller than or equal to an Indian state	33
B. All India	
(i) empirical—primary data	0
(ii) other	10
C. India plus another country	1
D. Not applicable	6
Total	50

Research into Social Differentiation has been primarily based on micro areal units of study. The majority of these articles were conducted in villages or a number of villages within particular states. In some cases though, especially if research was into the sociology of occupations and professions, research was carried out in urbanized areas. Research which considered all of India was predominantly empirical but utilized secondary data. Often attempts were made to determine the general state of caste system, for example what changes have the caste system undergone throughout all of India and to what degree has it continued to exist or disappeared. In a small number of articles, reference was made to federal government policies regarding the caste system and their success or failure. One article was exceptional in that aspects of caste hierarchy were viewed comparatively from India and the United States.

The topical emphases of the sociology of occupations and professions has reflected the changes which are occurring within the occupational structure of India. Increasingly studies have been conducted on occupational aspirations and mobility considering factors such as job, status, income, urban-rural differences, age, religion and education. In relation to mobility and aspirations, there have been studies in changes in occupational structure in villages as well as among particular groups such as castes or tribes. One of the earlier articles contained in the sample was a socio-economic survey of a particular occupational group. This type of research appears to be less popular as occupations have been studied more recently in light of their dynamics.

Social stratification has mainly consisted of research into the caste system. Emphasis has been placed on topics such as social stratification within micro units of study such as villages, tribe-caste continuum, social relationships between castes, the relationship between caste, class and power and the functional solidarity the caste system has provided to Indian society. A smaller amount of research has progressed into the study of caste councils and organizations, the status of castes as viewed sacredly and secularly and the working of caste allegiances within Indian politics. Most researchers appear to have agreed that the caste system is far from disappearing and that in spite of government efforts, still remains basically the same.

Summary of Important Trends : *Social Differentiation*

(1) Research in Social Differentiation has been based mostly on empirical, primary data, but empirical, secondary data as well as data from historical sources are important.

(2) Techniques of research most used are field work and surveys.

(3) Although the majority of research has been qualitative, quantification has become more common, especially for the testing of hypotheses.

(4) Theoretical developments have been limited with reliance on theoretical schemes based on Western thought or on ideal Varna system of caste.

(5) Emphasis has been on micro-analysis but generalizations have also been made for all of India in a moderate number of articles.

(6) Topical emphases has been placed almost solely on the caste system in social stratification and primarily on occupational structure, aspirations and mobility in the sociology of occupations and professions.

COMMUNITY STUDIES

Fifty articles classified as Community Studies have been analyzed to determine sources and method of data collection.

From Table 38 it is clear that community studies in Indian sociological research have been predominantly empirical, especially using primary data. All of the articles from the sample which dealt with communications, that is the adoption of new farming practices, were based on empirical, primary data. Approximately half of the articles dealing with urban areas were based on primary data whereas the other half mainly made use of secondary data. The vast majority of empirical studies using primary data were concerned with rural studies. Generally then, it appears that rural areas have been studied through the use of primary data whereas this is true to a lesser extent in urban areas. This discrepancy might be due to the complexity of urban living and problems which make field research more tedious and complicated. For example, the economy of a small relatively isolated village is more readily understood and analyzed than the economy of a larger settlement such as a city.

TABLE 38

Method of Data Collection	Number of Authors
A. Empirical Sources	
(i) primary data	30
(ii) secondary data	6
(iii) both primary and secondary data	3
B. Historical Sources	
(i) sacred	0
(ii) secular	2
C. Speculative—Philosophical	
D. Policy—Research	
(i) for government planners, etc.	0
(ii) for sociologists, anthropologists	4
E. Empirical—Speculative	2
F. Empirical—Historical	2
G. Speculative—Historical	1
Total	50

Policy research by sociologists has attempted to derive suitable frameworks for the study of rural society. The conclusion has been reached by many researchers that villages should be studied as a unit internally but in the final analysis must be integrated into a regional framework or that villages should be studied at their different levels of areal integration. Policy research by urban sociologists has not progressed to the same extent as that for rural studies. In community development likewise adequate frameworks have not been devised for the sociological study of projects although some research has been produced on evaluative studies.

Articles using historical material have obtained data from secular sources such as records of government legislation and programmes, accounts of India as a British colony and reports of early British administrators. Historical data was found to have been used solely for the study of rural society today and village life in the past. Articles which were speculative in nature attempted to outline possible reasons for the failure of rural programmes and offered new solutions to problems.

Research techniques used to collect empirical, primary data and their amount of usage are presented in Table 39.

TABLE 39

Research Techniques	Number of Articles
A. Field Research	8
B. Surveys	
(i) interviews	12
(ii) questionnaires	2
(iii) not specifically stated or both	9
C. Participant Observation	0
D. Records	0
E. Surveys and Records	0
Total	31

The survey technique, especially interviews, has been the most widely used tool in empirical studies of communities. Field research or the observation of community life by the researcher has been relatively of lesser importance. Those articles using field research were usually descriptive discussions of village life. Interviews and unspecified surveys were primarily rural studies and also a fewer number from communications and urban studies. The questionnaire was a major tool used by researchers in urban studies and commu- nications. The conclusion can be drawn that the phenomenon studied has had some influence on choice of techniques. The adoption of farm practices, for example, is more conducive to quan- tification as well as better analyzed through questionnaires and interviews whereas to obtain a descriptive analysis of a small rural village, field observation is perhaps a better technique,

The degree of quantification found in the articles was determined and the results are shown in Table 40.   The classes of amount of quantification are those referred to earlier.

TABLE 40

Degree of Quantification	Number of Articles
1	26
2	12
3	6
4	6
Total	50

Slightly over half of the articles included in the analysis were found to be qualitative.   Compared to the previous findings, however, for the subject areas of Culture and Social Structure and Social Differentiation, Community Studies have attained a significant orientation towards quantification.   Over 80% of the most quantified research (class 4) were articles on the communication and adoption of new farm practices.

Again the majority of articles in class 3 were concerned with aspects of innovation and change in agriculture.   There were also some analyses of rural social structure through the quantification of components such as family system, amount of education, material possessions, draught animals and others.

The two categories of least quantification were made up mainly of articles from urban and rural sociology and community development.   There does not appear to be any difference in studying rural or urban society in amount of quantitative research.   Community development research has been primarily qualitative often taking the form of critical analyses of government projects along with recommendations for the future.   Although community development projects have been evaluated quantitatively from an economic point of view, it appears that changes in social relationships and attitudes have not been accurately measured to any great extent other than using qualitative methods.

Out of the fifty sample articles, seven were judged to have some theoretical orientation. None of the seven had been classified as rural sociology but were from urban sociology, communications and community development. Within urban sociology there has been some progress made in the application of Western theories of urbanization and urban growth to the Indian situation or the situation of a developing economy. Much work however remains to be done. Often authors have researched urbanization assuming theoretical notions but not acknowledging this fact or attempting to prove or disprove the idea. In the light of the theoretical body of knowledge available concerning urbanization, urban growth and urban structures, it is surprising that more researchers have not tested and modified models with Indian data.

Some progress has been made in developing theoretical knowledge about adoption behaviour. Particular variables have been singled out over and over again as either aiding or hindering the adoption process. Stages of the adoption process have also been tentatively outlined. Reference has been made to similar studies and their findings carried out in other countries, particularly the United States. In spite of all this information however, which forms the basis of theory building, few researchers have begun to arrange this material or synthesize it into cohesive theories of the adoption process. As researchers have been making reference to theory and offering tentative theoretical conclusions, it can be expected that probably in the near future more substantial theoretical ideas will be forthcoming.

Finally, mention might be made of one article from the sample that was classed as a contribution to community development. The article was concerned with organizational strains in community development blocks and used organization theory as a basis for analysis.[16] Conclusions were stated not only in reference to India but also generalizing for societies at different levels of industrialization.

Rural studies have remained largely ideographic. This is perhaps understandable as problems are present in arriving at theories of Indian rural society because of the expansiveness of the country as well as its diversity. There is also the disadvantage of short-term research, often a result of funding schemes and other factors which limit time. In spite of these unavoidable barriers to theoretical developments much could be done by Indian sociologists to promote theories of rural society.   One gets the impression when examining articles on rural Indian society that research is quite disjointed as authors do not relate their findings to previous studies of the same nature.   The result is that findings remain isolated and the sets of interrelated propositions from which theories develop are lacking.

Hypotheses testing was a form of research used mainly by researchers in communications.   The pattern was generally followed where it was hypothesized which variables were related to acceptance or adoption of innovations and these hypotheses were then either accepted or rejected on statistical grounds.   Other instances where hypotheses were tested can be mentioned.   One article attempted to clarify the relationship between Islamic social structure and caste.[17]   It was hypothesized that Islam is an egalitarian religion and social stratification among the Islamic peasantry of India is entirely due to the Hindu caste influence.   The hypotheses was rejected in light of comparative data from other Islamic societies which were not influenced by the caste system but still exhibited caste-like social stratification.   Another article hypothesized that in spite of the census classification of a particular centre as 'urban', it was actually rural because of the attitudes and perceptions of the inhabitants.[18]   A third article started with the contention that the greatest number of migrants to urban centres would be caste members who had lost their function in the village and those in the weakest economic positions.[19]   In truth, it was discovered that migrants were usually upper caste members and land owners which disproved the hypothesis.

The areal perspective taken by authors has been determined and is shown in Table 41.

The results indicate that community studies in Indian sociological research have been primarily microscopic in approach. Considering the phenomena being studied it is not surprising that macro-level studies have been scarce as authors study one particular place in detail.   It might be contended though that over the past twenty-five years, the data collected for this analysis, indicated that enough work has been done of this nature.   Eventually, the data which has been collected at the micro-level should be related to a macro all-India framework based on empirical data.   There also has been a notable lack of cross-cultural studies between India and other countries as well as between communities in different parts of

India.   Hopefully, this avenue of research too will be pursued in the future so that valid generalizations can be made which apply to Indian communities and those of foreign countries.

TABLE 41

Areal Unit of Study	Number of Articles
A. Micro: any area smaller than or equal to an Indian state	35
B. All India	
(i) empirical—primary data	0
(ii) other	9
C. India plus another country	1
D. Not applicable	5
Total	50

The topical emphases of community studies has been on rural society, (80% of the same articles dealt with aspects of rural life). Villages were often examined in the totality of their social organization, economy and interactions.   Such studies tended to be descriptive in nature. Other rural phenomena though have also been the object of study such as rural migrations, industry, labour force, cooperative ventures, landholding and power structure.   Also a portion of research has been focused on rural education and reconstruction and development programmes of the government and the resultant changes.   A few articles examined criteria for the definition of communities as either urban or rural.

Urban community studies have examined processes of urban growth and urbanization, the reasons for urban growth and the role which larger centers come to assume within particular regions. Such research has stressed economic factors although social relationships have also been pointed out.   Recently more research has been conducted into social problems in urban areas such as social unrest and violence and poor standards of housing and general urban physical structures.   Some progress has also been made in the determination of urban characteristics which are distinct from rural characteristics such as land patterns and social institutions.

Communications as a part of Community Studies have entailed the adoption of new farming practices by rural inhabitants of villages. The acceptance of innovations has been studied in most cases by identifying factors which are positively correlated with adoption behaviour or negatively related. The roles of various people which are supposed to help in the adoption process such as village leaders, influential citizens, extension workers and others have been assessed. The conclusion has been reached by most researchers that economic considerations almost invariably outweigh traditional social factors in the decision to accept or reject an innovation.

Research in community development was generally found not to be of the case study variety but more generalizing and speculative. Often criticisms were made of development programmes and recommendations suggested by researchers with no accompanying statements on how their recommendations could be implemented. Organization of community development programme was analyzed considering it as a bureaucratic structure, where personnel become involved in various role conflicts. Research was conducted into the evaluation of community development on how to structure projects so that later progress can be measured or assessed.

Summary of Important Trends : *Community Studies*

(1) Community studies in Indian sociological research have been primarily concerned with rural communities.
(2) Communities have been studied mainly with the use of empirical, primary data that has been collected through questionnaires and interviews or surveys in general. Field research has also been utilized significantly.
(3) Research has been predominantly qualitative. The study of communications has been quite quantitative in contrast to the qualitative rural as well as urban studies.
(4) Theoretical knowledge about Indian communities has not been a concern of very many researchers. Although some progress has been made into theoretical concepts of urban areas and communications much work remains to be done.
(5) Areal perspective of research has been micro. Micro studies have not yielded significant all-India conclusions as most of

these studies have not been related to previous studies or to any theoretical framework.

THE FAMILY AND SOCIALIZATION

The subject area of the Family and Socialization includes the sub-categories of sociology of the child and socialization, adolescence and youth, sociology of sexual behaviour, sociology of the family and family planning. The data from the fifty sample articles was analyzed as to source and method of data collection. The classification scheme and results are presented in Table 42.

TABLE 42

Method of Data Collection	Number of Authors
A. Empirical Sources	
(i) primary data	37
(ii) secondary data	3
(iii) both primary and secondary data	1
B. Historical Sources	
(i) sacred	0
(ii) secular	1
C. Speculative—Philosophical	0
D. Policy Research	
(i) for government planners, etc.	1
(ii) for sociologists, anthropologists	1
E. Empirical—Speculative	2
F. Empirical—Historical	4
Total	50

From Table 42 it is known that research into the Family and Socialization in India has been mostly empirical using primary data and to a lesser extent empirical using secondary data and historical sources.

Articles classed as empirical using primary data were mainly from the sociology of the family and entailed the study of familial units or just husbands and wives through various techniques, which shall be mentioned later. Empirical studies using secondary data were all from the sociology of the family. The usual pattern was to establish basic concepts regarding the family in India and then discuss their various facets with comments on methodology, for example, an attempt was made to use marriage and its corresponding relations as a focal point for a consideration of kinship studies in India.

Historical data has had a minor role in the study of the family and socialization in India. In most cases particular phenomena have been discussed by presenting an outline of their history until the present day and supplementing this analysis with data collected in the field in modern times. Phenomena which were found in the sample to have been studied in this manner were prostitutes, polygynists, widow remarriage, dowry system and female infanticide. The historical data often provided the proper perspective necessary to chart changes in the phenomena due to a succession of various factors.

Policy research has been noticeably lacking in the Family and Socialization. One article attempted to offer advice to planners regarding the building of housing in order that family activities are provided with flexible and adequate space.[20] The recommendation was made that more research should be directed towards studying the interdependence of various factors relating to family life and the habitat. The article in the sample which was meant to be advice to sociologists was concerned with the responsibility of sociologists in researching specific problems in family planning because of India's drastic population problem.[21]

Research which was empirical and speculative was from the sub-category of family planning. One article speculated on how family planning could be made more effective as well as on the results of disparate birth rates and family size among different classes in Indian society.[22] Another article speculated also on how family planning could be made more effective as well as social complications which would follow because of differential adoption of different groups such as Hindus and Moslems.[23]

Empirical studies using primary data were further analyzed according to techniques used. The techniques and tabular data are shown in Table 43.

TABLE 43

Technique	Number of Articles
A. Field Research	8
B. Surveys	
(i) interviews	11
(ii) questionnaires	9
(iii) both or not specifically stated	4
C. Participant Observation	0
D. Records	
(i) census, data from other govt. surveys	4
(ii) newspaper advertisements	2
(iii) other	0
E. Public Opinion Surveys	2
F. Records (ads) and Interviews	1
G. Records (case histories) and questionnaires	1
Total	42

Survey techniques have emerged as being the most widely used technique in the Family and Socialization, with field research being of moderate importance. The use of survey techniques such as interviews and questionnaires by researchers might possibly be explained by the type of phenomena being studied A sociological analysis of aspects of family life must necessarily involve the examination of important facets which are not readily observable such as attitudes and inter-relationships. To discover such information family members must be questioned and allowed to discuss aspects of their conjugal and familial life.

Field research has generally been used for studies which tend to be anthropological in scope. Out of the eight articles classed as using this technique, six were from *Man In India* and *Eastern*

Anthropologist journals which contain anthropological and ethnological articles. Three articles were examinations of tribal family types and patterns and two were studies of widow remarriage where the extent of widow remarriage was determined and the ceremony of widow remarriages described.

Data provided by government sources was used in a small number of cases. Such data had been collected by the census the Indian Statistical Institute and the National Sample Survey. Matrimonial advertisements in newspaper has also provided data for analysis. Insights were obtained as to preferential characteristics of mates regarding variables such as occupation, education, caste affiliation and pre-marital status. Public opinion surveys were also found to be a useful tool by a few researchers. Public opinion surveys allowed authors to work with a large body of data without having to collect it themselves.

The sample articles for the Family and Socialization were analyzed according to degree of quantification. The results are shown in Table 44.

TABLE 44

Degree of Quantification	Number of Articles
1	15
2	14
3	19
4	2
Total	50

Compared to the other three subject areas which have already been discussed, the Family and Socialization was discovered to be quantitatively oriented. Although only a very small number of articles used statistical tests; from which to draw valid inferences, many used simple statistics and sampling procedures such as random samples and respondents chosen by referral or "snowball" technique.

Articles on family planning generally fell into class 2 or 3 although a few were found in class 1 and one in class 4. It appears that family planning research, which essentially is the study of the acceptance of a new innovation, has not used quantitative techniques to the extent to which they have been used for the study of the adoption of new farming practices and innovations. This is especially true when considering the limited use of statistical tests by family planning researchers. The usual format of research was to present statistics such as percentages and then draw conclusions from this data without tests of significance or correlation.

Articles which were classed as being qualitative, in almost all cases, had gathered data through field research or used secondary sources and non-empirical data. In contrast to this finding, as might be expected, articles which used higher degrees of quantification had gathered data through questionnaires, interviews and such survey techniques. It appears that the adoption of particular data gathering techniques has influenced researchers in their use of quantification in that some techniques provide sets of data which are more easily measured and tabulated than others.

Out of the fifty sample articles examined only three were considered to be contributions to theoretical knowledge on the family and socialization. Two of these articles were concerned with family planning. One based an analysis of family planning in India on the idea that the most important motivations for change are financial benefits and security.[24] It is believed that these motivators should be related to family planning so that once people are convinced of the economic, educational and health benefits they will become adopters. Another article on family planning made reference to theories of family planning adoption conceived of by Americans.[25] The main purpose of the article however was not to advance theoretical knowledge of family planning but to indicate areas that need research by sociologists.

An article from the sociology of the family was also found to make some contribution to theoretical knowledge in the form of typologies.[26] The author discovered after a critical review of census data followed by a study of 410 sample households that the distinction of "nuclear "versus" joint" family was not adequate. In other words, theoretically, these two family types exist but in reality many families do not fit these ideal types but should be classified somewhere between the two depending on the criteria used to make the decision.

The form of research where hypotheses are formulated and tested for acceptance or rejection has also been used quite infrequently by researchers in Family and Socialization. Out of the fifty articles only five had begun with a controversial idea and set out to prove or disprove it. Each of the four articles dealt with diverse topics although three were from the sociology of the family and one was from family planning. The article referred to earlier about census classifications of families as "joint" or "nulear" was one article which endeavoured to disprove a previously accepted idea. Another article on widow remarriage attempted to disprove the common notion that widow remarriage is in fact marriage or at least marriage in the sense of first marriage.[27] The authors show through examination of widow remarriage ceremony, that it is really more of a social alliance that is surrounded by secrecy and solemnity instead of public recognition and happiness.

A quantitatively oriented analysis of matrimonial advertisements structured five hypotheses at the beginning which in most instances could be numerically proved or disproved.[28] An example of such hypotheses is that the educated seek only educated people as spouses. Finally, one article on family planning hypothesized that females in the ante-natal, confinement and post-natal periods were ready targets of imparting family planning education.[29] The hypothesis was confirmed but also had to be modified to take into account new findings from the research. One article hypothesized as to the reason for sex delinquency and its relation to emotional instability.[30] The hypothesis was accepted that delinquents are more emotionally unstable.

The articles on the Family and Socialization were also analyzed as to areal perspective. The classification scheme and tabular findings are shown in Table 45.

Once again as with the other subject areas already discussed, studies in Family and Socialization have been primarily microscopic in approach. Generally, particular areas were sampled to yield samples of size 20 to 500 respondents in the form of married couples, households or only females, males, students and others. In one case data was used that surveyed 16,000 family units in rural Bengal but the data had been collected by the Indian Statistical Institute.[31] Micro or macro-level analysis did not appear to be significantly related to any particular subject area with the field.

TABLE 45

Areal Unit of Study	Number of Articles
A. Micro; any area smaller than or equal to an Indian state	35
B. All India	
(i) empirical—primary data	3
(ii) empirical—secondary data	3
(iii) other	1
C. India plus another country	3
D. Not applicable	5
Total	50

Three articles were classified as referring to all of India using primary data. At best this classification should be taken as tentative because none of the articles were extremely explicit on this matter. In one case a questionnaire had been mailed to 120 professors and teachers in India.[32] As the words "in India" do not indicate conclusively that data were drawn from every state or part of India, some caution must be exercised. Research topics for these empirical all-India studies were the dowry system, communication and motivation in family planning and general discussions of marriage in India. In another case, data from widespread parts of the country was gathered through public opinion surveys.[33]

Three articles found to be concerned with all of India used secondary data and were speculative and contained recommendations especially on the topic of family planning. Some comparative studies were found in the sample also. Three of them compared Indian responses to those of Americans regarding such things as vasectomy, matrimonial advertisements and attitudes towards children. Another article compared North Indian patterns of kinship and marriage to those of South India using hypothetical data as well as data from secondary sources.[34] The sociology of the family in India has tended to emphasize a variety of topics. Family types such as joint and nuclear have been studied as well as their organization and inter-relationships of members. From analyses of matrimonial advertisement considerable knowledge has been obtained on desirable traits in spouses and how the most sought after traits have changed through time. Widow remarriage has been the focus of interest of some authors, its attraction being mainly that remarriage appears to be an infraction of traditional Hindu law. The dowry system has also been studied, usually by viewing it as a social evil. Tribal marriage, family structure and kinship networks have been the result of anthropological investigations in the Sociology of the family. A considerable amount of research has gone into changes in family patterns and marriage in India such as intercaste marriages and the effects of education on family life. Finally, the family has been studied as it possibly will exist in future years and its present role as an institution in a rapidly changing society.

Family planning studies from the sample were concerned in the majority of cases with attitudes towards family planning, motivating family planning and the consequences of family planning on society. Family planning researchers also have come to the conclusion that people will adopt new innovations if the economic benefits of the innovation are clear to them. This finding is parallel to that discovered by researchers into the communication of farming practices. The sociology of sexual behaviour has studied deviant groups in society such as homosexuals and prostitutes as well as aspects of contraceptives such as socio-sexual factors in the use of oral contraceptives and factors influencing choice to adopt vasectomy.

Summary of Important Trends : The Family and Socialization

(1) Research in the Family and Socialization has been predominantly empirical using primary data. A moderate amount of research has been based on historical sources, especially coupled with some other form of empirical data.

(2) Data have been collected primarily through the use of survey techniques such as interviews and questionnaires.

(3) Data, in most cases, has been selected and manipulated with the use of simple statistics. More complicated quantitative techniques have been seldom used.
(4) Analysis of data has been usually undertaken with little consideration given to building theory or testing hypotheses.
(5) The majority of research has been microscopic in approach.

SOCIAL CHANGE AND ECONOMIC DEVELOPMENT

The subject area of Social Change and Economic Development consisted of the sub-categories of social change and economic development and market structures and consumer behaviour. Let us look at the methods and sources of data collection. Table 46 is a summary of the results.

TABLE 46

Method of Data Collection	Number of Articles
A. Empirical Sources	
(i) primary data	17
(ii) secondary data	9
(iii) both primary and secondary data	4
B. Historical Sources	
(i) sacred	0
(ii) secular	1
C. Speculative—Philosophical	5
D. Policy Research	
(i) for government planners, etc.	5
(ii) for sociologists, anthropologists	6
E. Empirical—Speculative	2
F. Empirical—Historical	1
Total	50

Social change and Economic Development in Indian sociological research was found to be less empirical than the other four subject areas previously analyzed, especially considering the use of primary data. Policy research and philosophical—speculative research was of greater importance than in other subject areas. Most of the articles classed as empirical using primary data were examinations of the nature and extent of changes among particular groups in India due to modernization. Development schemes as factors of social and economic changes were also the object of study.

Empirical research using secondary data was usually based on data and ideas of other authors which the researcher manipulated and went on making generalized statements or offered new conclusions about the findings. Articles using both primary and secondary data often utilized basic statistics provided by the census or district handbooks and then supplemented this with field research. Empirical-speculative articles used empirical data as the foundations of their arguments and then offered recommendations on how problems should be solved and what the results will be if their suggestions are implemented.

Policy research for government planners, administrators and legislators has revolved around the problem of modernization in India. The social consequences of economic development has been discussed to some extent and suggestions were usually made as to how harmful consequences might be mitigated or avoided. Opinions have also been expressed on the most effective way of bringing about change and the reasons for the slowness of change. Education for the masses emerged as the most agreed upon tool for social transformation.

Policy research for sociologists, social workers, anthropologists and other related social scientists primarily dealt with the problem of how best to study social change in India and which areas of study need more research so that practical problems of government may be partially solved. Most researchers appeared to agree that the study of social change in India can only proceed if the investigator is familiar with the traditions of India and puts his findings into historical perspective. It has also been considered important to view findings cross-culturally or at least to bear in mind that western concepts often are not applicable to conditions in India.

Research that was speculative and philosophical in nature usually examined social change in India in light of Hindu modes of thought and the applicability of western concepts about society to

India, social change in the hands of these authors at times becomes a question of moral change and ethics. Indian philosophy of life was examined in relation to economic growth, for example, Hinduism's ethical ideals appear to focus attention on spiritualism and other-worldly aspects. The truth of this statement was examined and related to economic growth.[35]

The empirical data using primary data was further analyzed to ascertain the techniques used by researchers. The results are shown in Table 47.

TABLE 47

Technique	Number of Articles
A. Field Research	17
B. Surveys	
(i) interviews	
(ii) questionnaires	
(iii) both or not specifically stated	
C. Participant Observation	1
(i) participant observation and survey technique	1
D. Records	
(i) census, data from other govt. surveys	2
(ii) other	
E. Public Opinion Surveys	
Total	21

Empirical research in the subject area of Social Change and Economic Development using primary data has generally been based on data collected through field research. Little use has been made of other techniques that were found to be popular with researchers in other fields. Studies which resulted from field research often were impressionistic in style. After a period of personal observation, authors related how they ascertained that villages and their inhabitants had changed. Changes were discussed considering the various aspects of village life such as economy, land holding systems, caste, occupations and joint family as well as attitudes of people. The general conclusion was reached that change has been slow and rather than being revolutionary, has been evolutionary.

The amount of quantification used by researchers was also analyzed for the articles classed as belonging to Social Change and Economic Development. Once again Chakrabarti's scale referred to earlier was used. The tabular results are shown in Table 48.

TABLE 48

Degree of Quantification	Number of Articles
1	47
2	3
3	0
4	0
Total	50

The data from Table 48 indicates that Social Change and Economic Development has been the most qualitative of the five subject areas chosen for indepth analysis. The lack of quantification stems from the fact that a fair proportion of research was policy research and speculative-philosophical research. Also the technique of field research which was used in most empirical studies to collect primary data does not yield the compiled knowledge in quantitative form but rather as qualitative statements.

Social Change and Economic Development appears to have been approached by Indian sociologists as a social philosophical controversy involving a confrontation of modernity and tradition. The problem does not appear to have been approached scientifically in order that a more concrete picture be created of the extent of changes as well as their effects. Many measures might be devised, not only in the form of simple statistics but also as scales or indexes, to measure more accurately than a subjective impression of the amount of changes which has come about. Attitudes of people towards modernization and how modernization has moulded these attitudes might also be pursued more quantitatively in order that the reality of this aspect of social change and economic development become clearer. Presently, it appears that attitudes are often determined by referring to the Hindu religious philosophy, for example the ideal of group action and cooperation versus individual action and competition. These two conflicting attitudes clearly have implications for economic growth. However, the extent of cooperative norms in India seems to be assumed on the basis of Hindu tradition instead of being empirically verified and measured.

Six articles out of the sample size of fifty were found to make use of theory and contribute to the building of theories. Four articles were based on western theoretical ideas. Marxist and Weberian models of modernization and relationship between religion and economic development have been criticized by Indian sociologists in light of the modernizing patterns found in India. One author went on to outline a theoretical framework for the study of modernization in India bearing in mind Hinduism's ethical ideals.[36]

Social change in the form of integration into the mainstream of society by tribal groups has generated some theoretical discussion. An integrative model was outlined by one researcher along with attendant social processes.[37] Another article on the unity of India in general used Radcliffe-Brown's concept of functional unity to define and describe Indian unity.[38] Using this point of view the author arrived at the conclusion that too much emphasis must not be placed on disintegrative aspects of conflict, since conflict does not necessarily mean disunity.

The four Purusharthas or goals of existence constituted an ideal basis of Indian society which allowed one researcher to examine Indian tradition and social change.[39] Western theories of change, however, provided the basis for another analysis which attempted to formulate a tentative model for organizational renewal, change and development.[40] Concepts developed by various foreign authors were assimilated into one model which was described as basically a synthesis of situation processes and techniques which have been found to characterise successful organization development programmes.

None of the fifty articles analyzed were structured in the form of hypotheses testing. Although a few articles began by offering controversial statements, they were not stated explicitly or proved or disproved in quantitative terms. For example, one author began with the idea that the Indian experiment in democracy was supposed to significantly change the social structure of villages.[41] After a period of field research in a village the author concluded that actual changes are less startling than what might be imagined.

The type of hypothesis testing, however, which the above example illustrates is not the kind that characterizes modern, empirical social research, especially from the United States. This form of hypothesis testing has not been adopted by researchers into social change and economic development in India. The lack is most likely related with the facts already mentioned such as the qualitative nature of research and the use of field research instead of surveys and other techniques which yield quantitative data.

The areal perspective taken by authors of the sample articles has been determined and the results tabulated and presented in Table 49.

TABLE 49

Areal Unit of Study	Number of Articles
A. Micro: any area smaller than or equal to an Indian State	20
B. All India	
(i) empirical—primary data	0
(ii) empirical-secondary data	11
(iii) other	4
C. India plus another country	1
D. Tribal Areas	
(i) empirical-primary data	1
(ii) empirical-secondary data	2
(iii) other	2
E. Not applicable	9
Total	50

Table 49 indicates that although the greatest proportion of studies have been at the micro-level, an almost equal number have been concerned with all of India. No all-India studies, however, have used primary data which might indicate that generalizations are being made about all of India without substantial empirical data to support generalities except from secondary sources. Micro-level studies on social change and economic development often have been concerned with tribal settlements and specific aspects of change such as development schemes, socio-cultural barriers to change, industrialization and political processes. It is surprising, though, that few studies were found to study villages in the totality of their changes and economic development. The comprehensive form of analysis used by rural sociologists to study village social structure and organization might profitably be used by researchers interested in social change in order that a better understanding be obtained of the dynamics of present day village India.

It is also disappointing that so few cross cultural comparisons of social change and economic development have been conducted. It is quite probable that much new knowledge could be gained about these processes if Indian data were compared to that collected from other developing countries. Interest in tribal societies in India seems disproportionate considering that tribal groups only make up a small percentage of the Indian population. The number of studies on tribals might be justified by the magnitude of their problems as they are not only being modernized, but also are becoming integrated in Hindu society. The authors' areal perspectives then have focused on tribal areas as separate entities within India because of the special problems facing these people.

Besides the topical emphases on tribal transition the nature and extent of social change throughout all of India has been stressed. Social change was often studied as a philosophy and as related to traditional Hindu thought. Social change and economic development appears from the sample to have concentrated on rural changes with few researchers examining this process within the urban context. Other aspects of social change and economic development have been studied such as the effect of conversion to Christianity on the economic development of people. One group was examined that had resisted change and thus were termed "static."

A moderate amount of emphasis has been placed on methods for studying social change in India as well as criticism of present programmes and their results. From conclusions reached by a variety of authors it appears that change is coming about very slowly, that the basic values of society have not changed and that people have relied too much on government initiative instead of their own. Researchers have often included recommendations although most of them have not been operationalized and probably will remain no more than ideas on paper.

Summary of important trends : Social Change and Economic Development

(1) Indian sociological research in the subject area of Social Change and Economic Development has been primarily empirical although, more emphasis compared to other subject areas, has been placed on policy research and speculative-philosophical research.

(2) Research has generally taken the form of impressionistic studies based on field research which are microscopic in approach or generalizing studies based on secondary data and speculation which are macroscopic in approach.

(3) Research has been overwhelmingly qualitative and non-theoretical. Most theoretical discussions have involved the use of western concepts.

(4) Hypotheses testing has not been used by researchers into Social Change and Economic Development.

References

1. B. Saraswati, "The Institution of Panji among Maithil Brahmans," *Man in India*, 1962, 42, 4, Oct.-Dec., pp. 263-276.

2. A.B. Bose and N.S. Jodha, "Some Observations on Factors Influencing Settlement of Households," *Man In India*, 1967, 47, 4, Oct.-Dec. pp. 272-278.

3. M.C. Goswami and D. N. Majumdar, "A Study of Social Attitudes Among the Garo," *Man in India*, 1968, 48, 1, pp. 55-70.

4. P. Chakrabarti, "Quantification and Social Research : A Trend Analysis," *Economic Weekly*, 1970, 5, 38, pp. 1571-75.

5. S.S. Sarkar, "Some Cultural Parallels among Australoids," *Man in India*, 1958, 38, 4, Oct.-Dec., pp. 296-300.

6. R.G. Fox, "Professional Primitives: Hunters and Gatherers of Nuclear South Asia," *Man in India*, 1969, 48, 2, April-June, pp. 139-160.

184 THE SOCIOLOGY OF CONTEMPORARY INDIA

7. L.P. Vidyarthi, "Urgent Anthropology for Tribal Bihar," *Journal of Social Research*, 1968, 11, 2, Sept. pp. 121-140.
8. N.K. Bose, "Cultural Relativism," *Man In India*, 1969, 49, 1, Jan.-Mar. pp. 1-9.
9. *ibid.*, and "Experiences in Cultural Enquiries" *Man in India*, 52, 3, 1972, pp. 201-212.
10. Y. Atal, "Professionalization of Sociologists", *Indian Journals of social Research*, 12, 2, August 1971, pp. 137-142.
11. P.M. Gardner, "Toward a Componential Model of Indian Caste", *Journal of Social Research*, 1968, 11, 1, Mar., pp. 37-48.
12. R.A. Schermerhorn, "A Tentative Theoretical Approach to the Study of Minorities in India," *Eastern Anthropologist*, 14, 1, 1961, Jan.-April, pp. 59-70.
13. K.K. Thakkar, "The Problem of Casteism and Untouchability,"*Indian Journal of Social Work*, 1956, 17, 2, June, pp. 44-48.
14. K.L. Sharma, "Caste and Occupational Mobility : A Study of A Village in Rajasthan," *Journal of Social Research*, 1967, 10, 1 Mar., pp. 26-32.
15. D.R. Chanana, "Studies on the Problem of Slavery Since the 17th century" *Indian Journal of Social Work*, 1958, 19, 3, Dec. pp. 203-209.
16. S. Dube, "Organizational Strains in the Community Development Blocks in India," *Indian Journal of Social Work*, 1968, 29, 2, July, pp. 135-146.
17. Z. Khan, "Caste and Muslim Peasantries of North India and East and West Pakistan" *Man in India*, 1968, 48, 2, Apr.-June, pp. 133-145.
18. B.R. Ghosh, "Naraina: An Urbanized Village," *Journal of Social Research* 1969, 12, 1, Mar. pp. 100-106.
19. E. Eames, "Some Aspects of Urban Migration From A Village in North Central India," *Eastern Anthropologist*, 1954, 8, 1, Sept.-Nov., pp. 13-26.
20. N. Viswanathan and M.M. Desai, "Housing and Family Life," *Indian Journal of Social Work*, 1966, 26, 4, Jan., pp. 393-405.
21. S.R. Mehta and M. Advani, "Sociology of Family Planning," *Indian Journal of Social Research*, 12, 2, August, 1971, pp. 123-127.
22. V.S. Mahajan, "Population Employment and Family Planning in India," *Indian Journal of Social Work*, 1961, 22, 3, Dec. pp. 253-257.
23. H.C. Ganguli, "A Psychological Analysis of the Family Planning Situation in India," *Indian Journal of Social Work*, 1968, 29, 3, Oct., pp. 233-242.
24. *ibid.*
25. S.R. Mehta and M. Advani, *op. cit.*
26. I.P. Desai, "The Joint Family in India—An Analysis," *Sociological Bulletin*, 1956, 5, 2, Sept., pp. 144-156.
27. B.C. Agrawal and M.A. Agrawal, "A Note on Natra : The So-called Remarriage among the Hindus of Malwa," *Eastern Anthropologist*, 25, 1, Jan.-April, 1972, pp. 73-81.
28. B.S.S. Rao, "A Study on Matrimonial Advertisements," *Indian Journal of Social Work*, 1969, 29, 4, Jan. pp. 379-388.
29. K. K. Kapil, "Promotion of Interspousal Communication on Family Planning as a Result of Educational Sessions in the Post-Natal Clinics," *Indian Sociological Bulletin*, 1965, 5, 4, Jul., pp. 215-220.

30. T.E. Shanmugham, "Sex Delinquency and Emotional Instability in Women," *Indian Journal of Social Work*, 1956, 17, 1, June, pp. 12-19.

31. K. Pakrasi, "A Study of Some Aspects of Household Types and Family Organization in Rural Bengal," 1946-1947," *Eastern Anthropologist*, 1962, 15, 3, Sept.-Dec., pp. 55-63.

32. G. C. Hallen, "Dowry System in India," *Journal of Social Research*, 1960, 1, 1, July, pp. 72-92.

33. J.S. Apte, "Communication and Motivation in Family Planning," *Indian Journal of Social Work*, 1965, 26, 2, Jul. 133-138.

34. L. Dumont, "Marriage in India—The Present State of the Question: III North India in Relation to South India," *Contributions to Indian Sociology* 1966, 9 Dec., pp 90-114.

35. M.S.A. Rao, "Religion and Economic Development," *Sociological Bulletin* 1969, 18, 1, Mar., pp. 1-15.

36. K.P. Gupta, A Theoretical Approach to Hinduism and Modernization of India, "*Indian Journal of Sociology*, 1971, 2, 1, Mar. pp. 59-91.

37. B.K. Roy Burman. "Some Dimensions of Transformation of Tribal Societies in India," *Journal of Social Research*, 1968, 11, 1, Mar., pp. 88-94.

38. T.N. Sheth. "A Note on the Unity of India," *Sociological Bulletin*, 1960, 9, 1, Mar., pp. 39-45.

39. D.P. Mukerji, "Indian Tradition and Social Change," *Economic Weekly*, 1955, 30, 7, 23, July, pp. 877-882.

40. R.P. Mohan, "A Preliminary Model for Organisation Renewal, Change and Development," *Indian Journal of Social Research*, 13, 3, Dec. 1972, pp. 179-193.

41. S. Trent, "Impact of Money Economy and Adult Suffrage on a Mysore Village," *Economic Weekly Annual*, 1956, 8, 3/4 and 5, Jan., pp. 101-104.

NINE

A Community of Sociologists

The intellectual orientation of any discipline and its modification through time is the product of a complex array of factors. These factors, to mention but a few, may stem from societal changes, scientific advancements, educational systems, social origins of practitioners, opportunities for employment and means of obtaining status. Because of the bearing that these factors have on the development of a discipline, examining the infrastructure of a discipline becomes important to understand "the state of the art" itself and its progress. This chapter attempts to examine a part of the complex inner workings of a particular discipline through adopting the conceptual framework of a "community of profession."[1]

The "community of profession" being studied here is the community of sociologists and scholars from related disciplines who have concerned themselves with the study of different aspects of Indian society. The analysis includes both sociologists and social anthropologists of Indian nationality as well as those from other countries, primarily the United States. Attention shall be focused on demographic characteristics, academic background, areas of specialization, current research, professional membership, employment patterns, honorary awards, sources of funding and productivity. Data were included on non-Indians because they have made substantial contributions to Indian sociology and because this allows comparisons to be made between the sub-groups, in relation to the foci of attention.

The conceptual framework of a "community of profession" used in the present analysis has its origins in William J. Goode's article "Community Within A Community: The Professions."[2] Goode identified groups of professionals as communities without physical locus. He cited several reasons why this use of the term community was appropriate for professional groups.   These reasons in brief are as follows :

(1) Its members are bound by a sense of identity.

(2) Once in it, few members leave so that it is usually a terminal or continuing status.

(3) Members share a set of values in common.

(4) Members of the community have role definitions for members and non-members.

(5) Members speak a common professional language among themselves, which is only partially understood by outsiders.

(6) The community exercises a certain degree of control over its members.

(7) The boundaries of the community are reasonably clear, though they are not physical and geographical, but social.

(8) Though the professional community does not produce the next generation biologically, it does so socially through its control over the selection of professional trainees, and through its training processes, it sends these recruits through an adult socialization process.

Thus the conceptual framework of a "community of profession" implies a socially and psychologically cohesive group within which there is considerable interaction based on one over-riding professional interest and where geographical location is unimportant.

The data for this analysis of a community of sociologists were obtained through using a detailed questionnaire mailed out in the second week of July, 1973. (A copy of the questionnaire is contained in the Appendix). The analysis presented here concentrates mainly on curriculum vitae or biographical data provided by the respondents.

A total number of 543 questionnaires were sent out, 424 to sociologists and people in related disciplines in India and 119 to those in other countries. The Indian mailing list was compiled from the 1972 edition of the *Commonwealth Universities Yearbook*. All those people who were listed as faculty members of departments of sociology and departments of social anthropology were recorded. A much lesser number of names were also drawn from lists of members of departments of social work, agricultural science (those teaching rural sociology) and social sciences. The list of names drawn from the *Commonwealth University Yearbook*[3] was supplemented by the names of sociologists working at other institutions such as the

Tata Institute of Social Sciences, the International Institute for Population Studies and the Gokhale Institute of Politics and Economics. The questionnaires were sent directly to the relevant persons in universities or institutes.

The names of the foreign contributors were drawn from our extensive bibliography of Indian sociological research. Names that occurred relatively frequently or those of authors of important works were listed. Addresses of these contributors were then obtained through use of the 1970 *American Sociological Association Directory*, *Who's Who in America* (*1973*) and *Scientific Men and Women in America*. If addresses still could not be found then journal articles or other publications by the authors were consulted, as the publications usually indicate authors' institutional affiliations.

Out of the 543 questionnaires mailed out, a total of 86 responses were received, 49 from India and 37 from other countries, yielding a response rate of 16%. Unfortunately, a number of the questionnaires were not filled out completely by the respondents. Many preferred not to fill out the curriculum vitae data and sent their own prepared biographical sketches. This procedure is understandable because it is much more convenient to the respondent and it would seem useless to spend time filling out a detailed questionnaire when all the information was already compiled. However, these curriculum vitae at times did not contain all of the information asked for in the questionnaire and made analysis of responses more cumbersome. Other respondents sent reports of their current research projects without biographical data (number=7), or were judged not to be contributors to sociological research (i.e. physical anthropologists, labour economists; number=7). One respondent, although a sociologist, made no contribution to sociological research and hence this case was excluded from our analysis.

Our methods of collecting data obviously have a number of limitations but because of a lack of information, there did not appear to be alternatives. It is very possible that only the more prominent foreign scholars have been chosen compared to the broader group of Indians sampled. It is difficult to ascertain if biases have been introduced because of non-response or if the sample is completely representative because of a lack of information regarding the total universe.

Respondents were first analysed according to particular demographic characteristics such as age, sex, marital status and number of children. Data of this nature is of value as it helps to identify to which segments of the population structure sociologists belong. The age structure of contributors is significant in that age is generally a variable which influences attitudes towards the discipline. Tables I and II show the age structure of Indian and foreign contributors.

TABLE I
Age Structure of Indian Contributors

Age Groups	Number
less than 29 years	6
30-39	15
40-49	13
50-59	4
greater than 60	0
not known	1
Total	40

Average Age = 38.8 years

TABLE II
Age Structure of Foreign Contributors

Age Groups	Number
less than 29 years	0
30-39	6
40-49	9
50-59	7
greater than 60	6
not known	3
Total	31

Average Age = 48.9 years

These tables as well as the average ages indicate that the Indian sub-community of sociologists is quite youthful, especially in comparison to the foreign sub-community. It is quite possible that the younger age structure of the Indian sub-community is due to the fact that it is only in the last ten to twenty years that sociology departments have become more widespread in Indian universities. It appears that sociology is attracting a sizeable number of students. The older average age of contributors not living in India is perhaps a reflection of a tendency for younger sociologists in Western countries to concern themselves with their own society. It is also possible that as India modernizes, it no longer holds the same attraction for young foreign scholars as an exotic or very different place to study.

The fact that the average age of sociologists in India is relatively young is encouraging for the development of sociology in that country. Previous studies[4] have concluded that young sociologists are agents of change within the profession because of their unique contact with social reality and their fresh encounters as compared to the experiences of older sociologists. Areas of specialization become modified or changed by novices in response to their perception of socio-cultural and socio-structural conditions. Sociology in India has been criticized as being overtly concerned with areas of study that have questionable relevance to critical modern problems. Perhaps with the advent of more younger sociologists, the scope of the discipline will be modified so that sociology can make a greater contribution towards analysing socio-cultural systems and solving the social problems of a country in transition.

TABLE III

Sex of Contributors

Sex	Indian	Foreign
Male	34	27
Female	6	4
Total	40	31

TABLE IV

Marital Status of Contributors

Marital Status	Indian	Foreign
Married	31	23
Single	5	2
Not known	4	6
Total	40	31

TABLE V

Average Number of Children of Married Contributors

Nationality	Average Number of Children
Indian	1.81
Foreign	2.24

The preceding tables offer a few more insights into the demographic characteristics of the community of sociologists and people in related disciplines that has studied Indian society. Table III reveals that the contributors have been overwhelmingly male. There does not appear to be any great difference between the sex ratio of the two sub-groups being analyzed, although foreign contributors have a slightly higher ratio of women to men. Tables IV and V indicate that contributors generally are married and have small families. The smaller family size of Indian contributors is possibly related to their younger average age, in that they are still in the process of producing children whereas foreign sociologists have finished this stage in the family life cycle. The small family size of Indian contributors might also be due to the fact that they generally have married in their late twenties (average age of marriage = 27.1 years).

TABLE VI

Academic Background of Contributors

Discipline	Indian	Foreign
Sociology	20.83	10.00
Socio-cultural Anthropology	2.50	10.50
Social work	1.91	1.00
Economics	2.75	1.00
Demography	2.75	1.00
Psychology	1.00	1.00
History, Literature	.58	1.00
Personnel Management	1.00	0
Statistics	5.66	0
Public Health	.33	0
Law	.33	2.00
Political Science	0	2.00
Linguistics	0	.50
Education	0	1.00
Other	.33	0
Total	39.97	31.00

The academic background of contributors was determined from the answers to question 2 in the curriculum vitae. Answers were generally reflective of the discipline or disciplines in which the respondent had taken his or her degrees. The tabulated data are presented in Table VI. One point was allowed for each respondent, that is, if a person stated that sociology was his or her discipline, then one point was added to the sociology category. When respondents indicated that they were trained in more than one discipline, for example demography and sociology, then each discipline was given a proportionate number of points. In the example, demography and sociology would have been each awarded .5 points. In a few other cases where respondents indicated 3 or 4 disciplines, .33 points and .25 points were allotted, respectively to categories.

In the Indian sample, research appears to be dominated by those people trained as sociologists. Of much lesser importance are people trained as demographers, statisticians, economists and socio-cultural anthropologists. This finding is encouraging for Indian sociology which in the past has been overshadowed by an emphasis on socio-cultural anthropology and analyses based on historical and sacred writings. These are also indications that sociological researchers in India have been receptive to the idea of interdisciplinary training in subjects which are complementary to sociology. Such training will probably allow researchers to work within a broader range of fields of interest and to use new methods, such as statistical analysis, thereby enriching the field of sociology.

Foreign contributors are primarily divided between sociology and socio-cultural anthropology. Comparison to the breakdown of Indian respondents might lead to the conclusion that the socio-cultural anthropological overtones of Indian sociology have been perpetuated more by foreign contributors than those native to India. The lack of foreign contributors trained in economics, demography and statistics could imply that foreign researchers have expended more energy studying those aspects of Indian society which they find very different from their own previous experiences, for example tribal groups.

Respondents were asked to name their chief fields of interest, this giving more insight into their academic orientation. The results are presented in Table VII.

TABLE VII

Chief Fields of Interest of Contributors

Category		Indian	Foreign
100	Methodology and Research Technology		
103	methodology (social science and behavioral)	.42	.25
104	research technology		
105	statistical methods		.25
200	Sociology: History and Theory		
202	of professional interest		

Category		Indian	Foreign
206	history and present state of sociology		
207	theories, ideas and systems		
300	Social Psychology	.50	.33
312	personality and culture	.25	
309	interaction within (small) groups		
322	leadership		
400	group interactions		
410	interaction between (large) groups		2.82
500	Culture and Social Organization		
508	Social Organization	.75	.83
513	culture	.50	.83
514	social anthropology (technology)	2.50	6.03
600	Complex Organizations		
621	industrial sociology	2.88	
623	military sociology		
624	bureaucratic structures		
700	Social Change and Economic Development		
715	social change and economic development	5.57	2.44
749	market structures and consumer behavior	1.00	
800	Mass Phenomena		
826	Social movements	1.17	
827	public opinion		
828	communications	.67	
850	mass culture	.33	
829	collective behavior		
842	sociology of leisure		
900	Political Interaction		
811	interaction between societies, nations, states		
925	political sociology		1.00
1000	social differentiation		
1019	social stratification	1.25	.45
1020	sociology of occupations		.33
1100	Rural Sociology and Agricultural Economics		
1116	rural sociology	.42	1.36
1200	Urban Structures and Ecology		
1218	urban sociology and ecology	.92	1.66
1330	Sociology of the Arts		

Category		Indian	Foreign
1330	sociology of language and literature		1.50
1331	sociology of art		
1400	Sociology of Education		
1432	sociology of education	1.74	1.58
1500	Sociology of Religion		
1535	sociology of religion	.42	
1600	Social Control		
1636	sociology of law		2.00
1653	penology and correctional problems		
1700	Sociology of science		
1734	sociology of science and technology		
1800	Demography and Human Biology		
1837	demography	8.83	1.05
1844	human biology		
*1845	family planning	2.25	.75
1900	The Family and Socialization		
1938	Sociology of the child and socialization		
1939	adolescence and youth	.58	
1940	sociology of sexual behavior		
1941	sociology of the family	.50	2.91
2000	Sociology of Health and Medicine		
2045	sociology of medicine (public health)	1.00	.33
2046	Social psychiatry (mental health)	.25	.25
2100	Social Problems and Social Welfare	.25	.33
2143	social gerontology	.17	
2147	social disorganization (crime)	1.58	.33
2148	applied sociology (social work)	1.41	.33
2151	delinquency	.83	
2200	Sociology of Knowledge		
2233	sociology of knowledge		
2252	history of ideas	.25	
2300	Community Development		
2317	sociology of communities and regions		.66
2400	Planning, Forecasting and Speculation		
2454	Planning and forecasting		
2500	Radical Sociology		
2555	radical sociology		

Category	Indian	Foreign
2600 Environmental interactions		
2656 environmental interactions		
2700 Studies in Poverty		
2757 studies in poverty	.33	
2800 Studies in Violence		
2856 studies in violence		
Total*	39.5**	29.9**

*   2 cases not known
**   figures are not even numbers because of rounded off decimals

The figures representing frequency of occurrence were calculated using a simple weighting system, because most respondents listed more than one field of specialization. For example, a respondent could conceivably list demography and rural sociology as his or her chief fields of interest; these 2 categories were then allotted .5 points each. The smallest amount allotted was .17 (1/6) and the largest 1.0 points. The number of points in each category were then added up to indicate the relative importance of particular areas. The classification system used was drawn from the *Sociological Abstracts*, 1972. An extra category was added for family planning.

Although the table is relatively self-explanatory a few of the more salient features may be briefly mentioned. Indian contributors appear to be highly oriented towards demography, social change and economic development, industrial sociology, family planning, the sociology of education and social problems and social welfare. The seemingly high position of demography is probably due to the structure of the Indian sample; approximately 25% of the respondents being employed at the International Institute for Population Studies. Among the foreign contributors, as might be expected, social anthropology was most highly rated. Also of importance were sociology of the family, group interactions, social change and economic development and the sociology of law. These results differ considerably from the findings of an earlier study[5] which attempted to identify trends in Indian sociology over the past twenty-five years. In that study contributors to Indian sociology

were found to be oriented towards social differentiation, rural sociology and sociology of the family. From this analysis, using more
current data, it appears that Indian sociologists are shifting their
emphasis to areas of research which are more closely related to
national, economic and social development. Foreigners, on the
other hand, are not following this trend to as great an extent as the
Indians, although they have given more attention to urban sociology, sociology of law and political sociology. The foreigners' interest in large groups has mainly taken the form of research into
international relations.

Researchers had a tendency to list more than one chief field of
interest. This was especially the case in the Indian sample, some
contributors listing up to six fields. It is difficult to draw firm
conclusions from this finding but a few might be suggested. It could
indicate that researchers are considerably flexible in their approaches
and display some broadmindedness. Such an orientation could
enrich sociological research as a more comprehensive understanding
of social reality could be the outcome. However, this does not
appear to be the case in Indian sociology. One respondent com-
mented that he felt "Individuals here and there conduct small
studies and they go on shifting their fields of interest, with the
result many of the studies conducted tend to be superficial and
impressionistic."

Trends in the dominant areas of specialization and research
can also be examined through the tables and findings of current
research projects. Productivity in terms of current research was
found to be much greater among the Indian sample; only nine
contributors (25%) in the Indian sample indicated that they were
not working on any specific current research project whereas 66%
of the foreigners were not currently engaged in sociological research
on India. The finding perhaps indicates that the role of foreigners
in Indian sociology is waning in terms of productivity. The
academic orientations of current research tend to support the
earlier findings regarding areas of specialization. Current sociological research in India was characterized by large numbers of
studies in demography, family planning, social problems and welfare, studies of youth and adolescence and community studies.
Foreign current research has placed emphasis on socio-cultural
anthropological studies, rural sociology, social stratification and
sociology of the family.

The academic qualifications of Indians and foreigners were found to differ. Only 19 out of 39 Indians (1 case was unknown) held a doctorate degree. These findings correspond somewhat to the age structure of both study populations, the older foreign researchers perhaps already having completed their doctorate programmes whereas some of the Indians were still at the predoctoral stage. However, an examination of the other 20 Indians with degrees at the masters level showed that only 4 appeared to be working towards their doctorates.

Eleven out of the 20 Indian researchers without doctorates though, held post-graduate diplomas and certificates in a variety of fields such as social service administration, demography, statistics, family planning and languages. No foreigners were holding diplomas of this nature. The certificates and diplomas are offered by institutions, for example, the International Institute for Population Studies (formerly known as the Demographic Training and Research Centre), the Tata Institute of Social Science, and the Indian Statistical Institute. This educational orientation of Indian sociologists will perhaps guide sociology in India towards a greater emphasis on practical problems and planning.

The vast majority of Indian contributors have been educated exclusively in India. Only six had studied elsewhere. These six had generally followed the pattern of obtaining their master's degree in India and then going abroad for doctoral studies. Those people who are of Indian origin but are living in other countries (counted as foreigners), were found to have also followed this pattern. Eight out of the nine contributors of Indian nationality who were living in other countries obtained their doctorates from universities outside of India. It appears then, that the probability of those students who received post-graduate education abroad, returning back to India is quite low.

An analysis of the universities that have granted degrees to contributors showed that there is not any strikingly dominant educational center. Indian universities which had granted the most master's degrees were Bombay, Agra, Lucknow and Poona. Non-Indian universities in this class were the University of Chicago, Stanford University, the University of Michigan, the University of California, Berkeley, the University of Illinois and Insitute for Social Science at The Hague. Leading institutes granting doctoral degrees were Bombay and Lucknow in India and Chicago,

California (Berkeley), Michigan, Yale and Oxford in the U.S.A. and U.K. respectively. In total, the University of Chicago has granted the most degrees among contributors, (5 masters and 8 doctorates) although a number of these degrees were in social anthropology.

An analysis of the professional membership of contributors was conducted in order to discover the cohesiveness of the community of profession and avenues for exchange of research information. Professional membership data can also show areas where different communities of professions overlap.

TABLE VIII

Professional Membership of contributors

Nationality	Total Number of Memberships	Average Number per Person	Number who belong to no Organization
Indian	56	1.5 (not known=13)	14
Foreign	172	6.2 (not known= 3)	1

Table VIII very clearly shows that foreign contributors have a much greater tendency to belong to various professional associations and societies. This is probably the case because of the greater opportunities available to join organizations in foreign countries compared to those in India as disciplines in foreign countries have been in existence longer and are more developed and organized. This trend is even more emphasized by the number of Indians who do not belong to any professional groups, (14 compared to 1 foreigner).

TABLE IX

Professional Organizations

Organization	Indian	Foreign
Indian Sociological Society	8	4
Indian Anthropological Association	3	1
American Anthropological Association	1	11
American Sociological Association	1	9
Indian Council of Social Science Research	5	
Association for Asian Studies	1	7

Organizations	Indian	Foreign
Royal Anthrop. Institute G.B. and Ireland	1	4
Current Anthrop.	3	4
Ind. Assoc. for Pop. Study	6	
Cdn. Soc. and Anthrop. Assoc.		8
Cdn. Assoc. for Asian Studies		2
Cdn. Society for Asian Studies		2
Rural Sociological Assoc.		3
Natl. Council on Family Relations		3
Royal Asiatic Society		2
Intl. Sociological Assoc.	1	3
Intl. Sci. Commission of the Family		2
Amer. Oriental Society		3
Linguistic Society of America		2
Intl. Assoc. for Tamil Studies		2
Amer. Psy. Assoc.		2
Ind. Psy. Assoc.	1	2
Pop. Assoc. of America	1	1
Society for Applied Anthrop.		3
Amer. Ethnological Society		2
Sijma X :	1	4
Dravidean Linguistic Assoc.		2
South West Anthrop. Assoc.		2
Sociological Research Assoc.	1	2
Society for the study of Social Problems		2
Intl. Union for the Sci. Study of Pop.	2	1
Amer. Assoc. of University Professors		2
Conference Intl. de Soc.		2
Amer. Academy for the Advancement of Science		3
Amer. Assoc. for Asian Studies		2
Ethnographic and Folk Culture Society (U.P.)	1	1
Ind. Folklore Assoc.	2	
Ind. Science Congress	2	
Assoc. of Schools of Social work (India)	2	
Bombay Statistical Society	2	
Other*	11	56
Total	56	172

*Those organisations with a total frequency=1.

Abbreviations Used in Table IX
G.B.   = Great Britain
Anthrop. = Anthropological; Anthropology
Ind. = India
Assoc. = Association
Pop. = Population
Cdn. = Canadian
Soc. = Sociology
Natl. = National
Intl. = International
Sci. = Scientific
Amer. = American
Psy. = Psychological
U.P. = Uttar Pradesh

Table IX shows the most important professional organizations according to the number of members found in the sample. All those organizations which had two or more respondents as members were listed. The important Indian Organizations appear to be the Indian Sociological Society, the Indian Association for Population Study, the Indian Council of Social Science Research, Current Anthropology and the Indian Anthropological Association, while the most important foreign organizations are the American Anthropological Association, the American Sociological Association, the Canadian Sociology and Anthropology Association, and the Association for Asian Studies. Unfortunately, there are only a few organizations which have substantial membership from both India and abroad as such grounds for meeting could prove to be a valuable vehicle for promoting the exchange of ideas and international research collaboration. Two notable organizations which have substantial Indian and foreign membership are the Indian Sociological Society and Current Anthropology. Closer examination of the Indian sample showed that approximately one-third of the memberships were with foreign or international organizations indicating, perhaps, that there is a vital need for more sociological organizations in India.

Foreign researchers, as might be expected from their academic background belong to a higher percentage of anthropological associations compared to Indians. The foreigners do not appear to be organized among themselves by any central interest in India but belong to groups whose members' interests are more broad or diffused such as Asian studies or areas of specialization such as the family or social problems. This situation again, may not be conducive to fruitful communication among scholars interested in the study of Indian society and culture. Hopefully, in the future more professional societies will be created in India and greater efforts will be made by professional organizations to attract members from both India and abroad.

The questionnaire had also asked that respondents provide their employment history. Although the analysis was at times hampered by incomplete data some preliminary conclusions may be drawn. The general pattern followed by both foreigners and Indian contributors was employment as teachers in universities, beginning with lectureships or employment as research assistants. Promotions were then usually obtained to assistant professor, associate professor or reader, full professor and in a few cases professor emeritus. This hierarchy was usually interrupted by visiting lectureships, other research activities and projects and consultantships or extra-university employment such as a case-worker, community organizer, statistician or psychiatrist. It appears that the hierarchy from lecturer to full professor is more dispersed with these other activities in the case of foreigners compared to Indians. Approximately one-half of the Indian sample were found to have worked at jobs besides their teaching duties while two-thirds of the foreign sample had had this experience. It was also noticed, although data were incomplete for more careful analysis, that Indian scholars generally took a longer time to reach the rank of full professor. This is probably because of the promotion system in Indian universities, that is, promotions usually come about only if a higher position is vacated, whereas in universities abroad promotion comes about regardless of the state of other positions in departments.

In order to gain some insight into the mobility of contributors the average number of appointments or jobs held throughout a career was calculated as well as the average number of locations of the employment. Foreigners were found to have had an average of 8.2 appointments while Indians had only 2.9. The average number of geographic locations where contributors had found employment was 5.9 for foreigners and 1.9 for Indians. In total it appears that foreigners have more vertical social mobility and geographical mobility compared to Indians. It also appears that there are limited opportunities for Indian sociologists to change this situation as new jobs are not that widely available with research institutions and government agencies. It is perhaps such conditions of limited opportunities for upward mobility and lack of diversity in experience, which have contributed to the migration of Indian sociologists to other countries and to making sociology in India more academically oriented than practical in nature. As a consequence, valuable human resources are lost and research needed to aid the country in development and modernization is not available. A word of caution though, should be interjected, i.e. that the sampling method used here has very possibly led to a more selective representation of foreigners, that is, the ones that are relatively well-known while the Indian sample included a broader range of contributors. The age factor is also worthy of note here, foreigners being on the average ten years older than the Indians. These factors must be taken into account in relation to the conclusions reached about the differences in employment patterns between foreigners and Indians.

Although the data from the questionnaire were found to be incomplete, some conclusions may be reached regarding the eminence of members of the community of interest here as well as their sources of funding. Very few respondents were found to have been recipients of honorary degrees; only one person being found in each of the sub-communities of foreign and Indian contributors. However, a larger number of researchers had received various national and international awards. The six recipients of awards from the Indian sample had received honours in the form of medals and prizes from universities, memorial awards, awards from the government of India for services and directorships or presidencies of academic societies and institutions or being made honorary fellows or members of these organizations. Five people were found in the foreign sample who had been recipients of noteworthy awards. These awards had been mainly granted by American universities for long years of service or exceptional research and publications. One researcher, an Indian by nationality but living in the United States received a number of distinguished awards for his work in demography, and family planning in India. On the whole, it appears that a number of people highly placed in the academic world have contributed to Indian sociology, although awards and honours to sociologists have been limited.

In this respect, the community of profession appears to have some cohesiveness, rewards coming from within the group instead of from external sources.

The analysis showed that the sample of foreign scholars had received approximately four times as many post-doctoral fellowships and research grants as the Indian sample. This funding clearly shows the financial restraints that many Indian researchers are forced to contend with, and could perhaps explain why contributors in teaching positions may be reluctant to accept research projects. The vast majority of post-doctoral fellowships and grants received by Indian contributors was from sources outside of India, particularly the United States. They were usually grants from American universities, such as Chicago, Stanford and Michigan' and research funding agencies such as the Rockefeller Foundation and the United Nations. Foreigners received grants from a number of universities and institutions and foundations. The most prominent universities which had funded research were American ones, such as the universities of Chicago, Wisconsin, California (Berkeley), Illinois and Duke and Mississippi State Universities. The Universities of British Columbia, Calgary and Lethbridge were Canadian institutions which had financed research. A larger amount of financial aid though appears to have come from sources other than universities. Some of the most important agencies were the Rockefeller and Ford Foundations, the Social Science Research Councils of Canada and the United States, The American Institute for Indian Studies, the National Science Foundation, the Canada Council, the American Council of Learned Societies and the Werner-Grenn Foundation for Anthropological Research.

Further analysis of funding sources was possible through examining sources of funds for current research projects when it was indicated. In the Indian sample, the Indian Council of Social Science Research was found to be the most important source of funds. Various universities had also provided money for research as well as government agencies such as the Planning Commission. The International Institute for Population Studies was conducting a number of research projects as a part of their normal work, while a few respondents mentioned that their source of funds was from their personal resources, especially if they were doctoral candidates. A number of the foreign contributors were not working on any specific research project at the time of the question-naire but sources of funding indicated were institutions devoted to Asian studies, the Ford Foundation and the universities with which the researchers were affiliated. In conclusion, the Indian contributors appear to have been financially quite handicapped as compared to those in the foreign sample.   This condition has no doubt had a detrimental effect on the development of sociology in India because of the difficulties involved in obtaining funds for research.

The productivity of members of the community of contributors to Indian sociological research was measured through the use of a crude productivity index.   The index was based on the allotment of points to different types of publications.   The following scheme was used.

Type of Publication	Number of Points
1. Research and Theoretical Monographs (Books)	30
(i) co-authorship	15
2. Text-books	15
3. Edited books	10
(i) co-editorship	5
4. Article in an edited book	10
5. Paper presented at seminars, etc.	5
6. Research Reports	10
7. Census Reports	10
8. Translations	5
9. Bibliographies	5
10. Not known	5
11. Articles in :	
(i) *Sociological Bulletin*	10
(ii) *Man in India*	10
(iii) *Journal of Social Research*	10
(iv) *Indian Journal of Social Work*	10
(v) *Eastern Anthropologist*	10
(vi) *Indian Sociological Bulletin*	10
(vii) *Contributions to Indian Sociology*	10
(viii) *Indian Journal of Social Research*	10
(ix) *Economic and Political Weekly (Economic Weekly)*	10
(x) *Indian Journal of Sociology*	10

Type of Publication	Number of Points
*(i) *American Sociological Review*	10
(ii) *American Journal of Sociology*	10
(iii) *Social Forces*	8
(iv) *Sociometry*	8
(v) *British Journal of Sociology*	7
(vi) *Social Problems*	7
(vii) *Public Opinion Quarterly*	7
(viii) *Demography*	6
(ix) *Rural Sociology*	6
(x) *Administrative Science Quarterly*	6
(xi) *Journal of Marriage and the Family*	6
(xii) *Milbank Memorial Fund Quarterly*	6
(xiii) *American Sociologist*	6
(xiv) *Sociology of Education*	5
(xv) *Sociological Quarterly*	5
(xvi) *Journal of Health and Social Behavior*	5
(xvii) *Social Science Quarterly*	5
(xviii) *Sociology and Social Research*	5
(xix) *Sociological Inquiry*	5
(xx) *Pacific Sociological Review*	5
(xxi) *Sociological Analysis*	4
(xxii) *Phylon*	4
All other journal articles	5

* Rating system for American journals (i—xxii) taken from N.D. Glenn and W. Villemez, "The Productivity of Sociologists at 45 American Universities", *American Sociologist*, 5, August, 1970, pp. 246. Unpublished research was allotted equal points with published research of the corresponding type ; if it was not known or indicated which form the publication would take then 5 points were allotted.

Credit work for degrees, diplomas, certificates, etc., was not counted unless the work had been published in some other form.

The preceding scheme was in part derived from the article by N.D. Glenn and W. Villemez, "The Productivity of Sociologists at 45 American Universities."[6] Glenn and Villemez outlined a method for ascertaining the productivity of American sociological research. A sample of sociologists were asked to assign weights to different types of publications and to rate the importance of different American journals. The median values were then calculated for each type of publication. The publications of members of Departments of Sociology at American universities were then weighted according to the scheme to yield a comprehensive index of departmental productivity. In this analysis it was not possible to use a sample of sociologists to assign weights; therefore, Glenn and Villemez scheme was used when possible. Additions had to be made for research reports, articles in edited books, bibliographies, translations, census reports and papers presented at seminars. Indian sociological journals also had to be assigned weights. The most important journals were equally assigned a weight of 10 points each. In the absence of an Indian study similar to the one by Glenn and Villemez we adopted this procedure since ranking of Indian journals would have been arbitrary without a representative sample of opinions from Indian and foreign sociologists regarding ranking of journal's published in India.

The work of foreign contributors was given points only if the publication had relevance to Indian society. Data was generally found to be complete, although a few respondents sent only lists of their most important works or selected bibliographies.

TABLE X

Productivity of Contributors

Nationality	Total Number of Points	Average Number per Contributor
Indian	7546	203.9 points
Foreign	6424	194.7 points

As shown in Table X, the average productivity indices of Indians and foreigners were 203.9 and 194.7 points respectively. The Indian sample ranged from 15 to 1495 points and the foreign sample from 35 to 780 points. It appears, therefore, that the Indian sample has been slightly more productive than the foreigners at least in terms of sociological research in India. It must be pointed out, however, that if all the research done by the foreign sample on any topic was calculated it would exceed the amount of research done by Indians greatly. Thus in total the foreign researchers have been more productive than the Indians. Considering that many of the foreign researchers have done additional research in areas other than Indian sociology, their productivity rating is surprisingly high. The sample age structure however, probably has some bearing on these results, that is, that the older foreigners have been involved in research for a greater number of years. The findings regarding productivity also confirm previous statements that research in India is wrought with difficulties such as inadequate funds and facilities.

Table XI

Regional Distribution of Respondents and their Productivity (*Indians*)

Region	Number of Indian Respondents	Total Productivity
Jammu and Kashmir	0	0
Himachal Pradesh	1	445
Assam	1	not known
Punjab	1	330
Haryana	0	0
Rajasthan	1	235
Gujarat	1	95
Maharashtra	19	1791
Madhya Pradesh	1	50
Uttar Pradesh	6	490
Bihar	2	1690
West Bengal	2	not known
Orissa	1	100
Andhra Pradesh	1	105
Karnatak	3	705 (one not known)
Tamil Nadu	0	0
Kerala	0	o
Delhi	2	450
Not known	1	1060
Total	42	7546

The above table shows the regional distribution of Indian respondents. It appears from the data that sociological research has been overwhelmingly conducted by scholars working in Maharashtra. This in fact, is due to a bias in the sample because of the very good response from the staff of one research institute in Bombay, (12 out of the 19 people from Maharashtra). However, the importance of this province as a center for sociological research should not be underestimated. Also of importance are the research centers in Uttar Pradesh, and to a lesser extent those in Karnatak, Bihar, West Bengal and Delhi. Areas of under-representation are North West India, (Gujarat, Rajasthan, Jammu and Kashmir, Punjab, Himachal Pradesh) and Eastern India (Tamil Nadu, Andhra Pradesh, Orissa).

In terms of productivity, the most important provinces appear to be Maharashtra, Bihar, Karnatak, Uttar Pradesh and Delhi. Again North-Western and Eastern India are unrepresented.

In the foregoing we have examined a community of profession, consisting of those scholars who have studied India from a sociological point of view. The important conclusions can be summarized as follows.

(1) The average Indian contributor is in his late thirties, married and has generally two children. This same situation holds for foreigners, although they are on an average ten years older.

(2) Indian contributors have been primarily trained as sociologists and to a much lesser extent as economists, demographers, and statisticians; foreigners have been trained equally as social-cultural anthropologists and sociologists.

(3) Chief areas of specialization for Indians were demography, social change and economic development, industrial sociology, family planning, sociology of education and social problems and welfare. Chief areas of specialization for foreigners were socio-cultural anthropology, sociology of the family, group interactions, social change and economic development and the sociology of law.

(4) Foreign contributors had had more academic training than Indians, although a number of Indians also had taken professional degrees, diplomas and certificates. Most Indians had been educated exclusively in India. Those that had gone

elsewhere for doctoral studies exhibited a strong tendency not to return to India.

(5) Indians belong to considerably less professional organizations and there is limited overlap between organizations to which both sub-groups belong.

(6) Compared to foreigners, Indians appear to have limited employment opportunities in terms of upward social mobility geographical mobility and types of employment available outside of universities.

(7) A number of honoured scholars have studied Indian Society, although awards appear to be mainly from the academic world. Financial aid for research was shown to have been much easier to obtain in the case of foreign contributors.

(8) Foreigners and Indians appear to be approximately equally productive in terms of Indian sociology, although foreigners have been much more productive in terms of total research output.

(9) Most productive regions in India are Maharashtra, Uttar Pradesh, Karnatak, Bihar and Delhi.

References

1. William J. Goode, "Community within a Community: The Professions," *American Sociological Review*, vol. 22, 1957, p. 194.
2. *ibid.*, pp. 194-200.
3. *Commonwealth Universities Yearbook*, 1972, London : The Association of Commonwealth Universities.
4. N. Stehr and L.E. Larson, "The Rise and Decline of Areas of Specialization", *American Sociologist*, 7, 7, August, 1972, pp. 3-6.
5. Marshall, B. Clinard and Joseph Elder, "Sociology in India : A Study in the Sociology of Knowledge"' *American Sociological Review*, 30, August, 1965, pp. 581-587.
6. N.P. Glenn and W. Villemez, "The Productivity of Sociologists at 45 American Universities", *American Sociologist*, 5, August, 1970, pp. 244-252.

APPENDIX
SURVEY OF CURRENT SOCIOLOGICAL RESEARCH IN INDIA
(1968)

N.B. : (1) Report each project on a separate form

(2) Attach additional sheets if necessary.

1) Project title :

2) Person (s) conducting research :

3) Objects of study (problem/hypothesis) :

4) Sample and Research Methods :

5) Summary of major findings : (please attach separate sheet)

6) When was the research started :

7) When was it completed :

8) If research is in progress probable date of completion :

9) Publication details : Place of Publication, Publisher, Year of Publication

    a) Book

       Article

       Other (specify)

    b) Unpublished : microfilm/mimeograph/other (specify)

10) Is publication of the results planned :

11) What form is the publication expected to take :

12) Source of finance for this research :

13) Research : Pre/Post/Doctoral/Other (specify) :

14) Problems experienced in conducting research : (please attach separate sheet)

15) International research collaboration (if any) :

16) Any other related comments on sociological research in India : (please attach separate sheet)

17) Address of researcher :

Please return this form by *airmail* to :

D. A. Chekki, Department of Sociology
University of Winnipeg
515 Portage Avenue, Winnipeg, Canada
R3B 2E9

CURRICULUM VITAE

Please prepare your biographical data providing information on the following items : (attach additional sheets if necessary)

1) Full name :

   Place and date of birth :

   Marriage data :

   Number of children :

2) Discipline : (Sociology/Anthropology/Psychology/Social Work/ Other (specify))

3) Education : (earned degrees and diplomas with colleges, universities and dates)

4) Honorary degrees with universities and dates :

5) Post-doctoral fellowships grants :

6) Past and present full-time employment :

7) Positions held concurrently with full-time employment, e.g. lectureships, consultantships, and appointments to national commissions etc.

8) National and international scientific honours and awards :

9) Membership in national and international scientific societies :

10) Chief fields of research interest :

11) Publications : (please attach separate sheet (s))

12) Titles of unpublished research : (please attach separate sheet (s))

13) Nationality :

14) Address :

Please return this form *by airmail* to :

D. A. Chekki, Department of Sociology
University of Winnipeg, 515 Portage
Avenue Winnipeg, Manitoba, R3B 2E9
Canada

Index

Ahmed, Imtiaz 15-20
America (*also* United States) 10, 33, 43, 50, 90, 94-101, 110, 119, 143, 158, 159, 164, 181, 186, 199, 204
American: doctoral dissertations 4; influence 18, 89; scholars 50, 89; sociological thought 17
Analysis : organisational framework of 2; of empirical survey 3
Anthropological field study 97
Anthropologists 58; 65, 152
Authors : 88; British 95, 96; female 107, 108; male 107, 108; nationality of 95

Banerjee, G.R. 44
Beteille, A. 32
Bibliographic entries 2, 7, 10, 12, 145
Bottomore, T.B. 15-18
Britain (*also* UK) 10, 58, 89, 90, 92, 94, 95, 98-102, 143, 179
British : influence 18, 89; scholars 89; society 29; sociological anthropology 17; sociological journals 15, sociology 15, 17
Bureaucratic structures 46

Caste : groups 29, 50; system 32, 36, 68, 154, 155, 157-59, 165
Chakrabarti, P. 19, 149, 179
Chandrashekhar, S. 39, 40
Changing role of women 32
Christianity 56, 57, 153, 182
Classification : of authors 12; process 8
Clinard, M.B. 15, 16, 18, 19, 52
Cohen, Stephen P. 47
Collective : bargaining 48; behaviour 43
Community : development 7, 25, 50-53, 93, 96, 102, 106, 110, 119, 124, 127, 144, 145, 163, 164, 167; programme 18; projects 52
Complex organisations 25, 93, 97, 102, 119, 124, 127, 128, 139, 144
Conflicts in industry 47
Cross : classifications 119; classified entries 9; cultural comparisons 34;

disciplinary study 103: tabulations 118, 127
Cultural : anthropology 6, 89; conflict 29; contact 29; integration 29
Culture : and social life 29; and social structure 23, 24, 28, 93, 95, 118, 119, 124, 126, 127, 139, 142, 144-47, 149-51, 153, 156, 163
Current anthropology 201

Data : classification 118; collected 6, 128; collection biased 1; collection, method of, 16, 147, 154, 168; collection techniques 3, 65; quantitative 3
Delhi : 130, 138-40; pilot project 52
Demography and human biology 25, 38, 39, 93, 95, 96, 102, 106, 124, 139, 144, 195
Developing : economy 36, 164; society 65
Development : of sociology 107; plans 92
Doctoral dissertations, 10, 113, 117, 119
Dube, S.C. 15, 19
Dumont, L. 15, 32, 93

Ecological studies 54
Economic : development 54, 66; 68, 97, 100, 102, 118, 127, 128, 142, 177, 196; policies 66
Educational reforms 51
Education : adult 51; primary 51; social 51; tribal 51; university 51
Elder, Joseph W. 15, 16, 18, 19
Environmental interactions 27, 68, 69, 95, 100, 105, 126, 144
Evaluation programme 92

Family and socialisation ´24, 28, 93, 145, 168, 172, 173, 175, 195
Family planning : 7, 38, 169, 170, 171, 172-75, 195-98, 203, 209; programme 39; research 39; surveys 65
Female authors 32
Foreign : authors 92; collaboration 92, 143; sociologists 23

LIBRARY OF DAVIDSON COLLEGE

Books on regular loan may be checked out for **two weeks**. Books must be presented at the Circulation Desk in order to be renewed.

A fine is charged after date due.

Special books are subject to special regulations at the discretion of the library staff.